T0380291

# ANGELS *and* MIRACLES

## MY WALK THROUGH LIFE WITH GOD

# PRINCE ALBERT WILLIAMS

WESTBOW
PRESS®
A DIVISION OF THOMAS NELSON
& ZONDERVAN

WestBow Press books may be ordered through booksellers or by contacting:

WestBow Press
A Division of Thomas Nelson & Zondervan
1663 Liberty Drive
Bloomington, IN 47403
www.westbowpress.com
844-714-3454

ISBN: 979-8-3850-2358-5 (sc)
ISBN: 979-8-3850-2359-2 (hc)
ISBN: 979-8-3850-2360-8 (e)

Library of Congress Control Number: 2024907603

Print information available on the last page.

WestBow Press rev. date: 05/31/2024

# Contents

# Contents

# GOD SAID, "WITNESS."

I said, "How?"

God said, "Tell them what I have done for you, tell them about Jesus, tell them that His blood alone can set them free, tell them the plan of salvation."

Take up your cross
and follow me
Prince Albert
Kingdom of God

"So, it will be at the end of the age. The angels will come forth, separate the wicked from among the just, "and cast them into the furnace of fire. There will be wailing and gnashing of teeth." (Matthew 13:49-50 NKJV)

# Acknowledgments

To my dear, sweet niece, Kathy Burfield, I appreciate the contributions you have made to this book and the love you have for me.

To Bobbie Murphy, my wonderful, darling, first granddaughter. I am grateful to you, for without your help, this book may not have been made! You inspired me. I love you.

To Katelyn Defreeze, my loving great-granddaughter, you have been a very big blessing from the time you came into my life.

To my darling daughter Kathy and my son-in-law Mark, thank you for making my last years on earth so easy.

And I am thankful for the input of several family members and friends.

As to friends, I have two special friends that have been a great help to me with my grammar, punctuation, and flow of my story line.

To my loving family, I believe God has inspired me to leave you something far more important than money or anything I have done in my life. This book is a record of my undying love for you. You are blessed. Thank you for the great love you have shown to me.

To you, my dear readers, may I, Prince Albert, be your loving friend, and I hope to meet you in heaven.

# Introduction

The following piece is from an unknown source. I find it to be oh-so-true.

## And Then It Is Winter

You know… time has a way of moving quickly and catching you unaware of the passing years. It seems just yesterday that I was young, just married, and embarking on my new life with my mate.

Yet in a way, it seems like eons ago, and I wonder where all the years went. I know that I lived through them all. I have glimpses of how it was back then and of all my hopes and dreams.

But here it is… the winter of my life, and it catches me by surprise…. How did I get here so fast? Where did the years go? And where did my youth go?

I remember well seeing older people through the years and thinking that those older people were years away from me and that winter was so far off that I could not fathom it or fully imagine fully what it would be like.

But here it is, my friends are retired and getting gray, they move slower, and I see an older person now. Some are in better and some worse shape than me… but I see the great change… These people are not like the ones that I remember, who were young and vibrant… but, like me, their age is beginning to show, and we are now those older folks that we used to see and never thought we'd be!

Each day now, I find that just getting a shower is a real target for the day!

And taking a nap is not a treat anymore… it's mandatory! Cause if I don't sleep of my own free will… I just fall asleep where I sit!

And so… now I enter this new season of my life unprepared for all the aches and pains and the loss of strength and ability to go and do things that I wish I had done but never did!

But at least I know, that though the winter has come, and I'm not sure how long it will last… this I do know, that when it's over on this earth… it is not over. A new adventure will begin!

Yes, I have regrets. There are things I wish I hadn't done… things I should have done, but didn't, and, indeed, there are many things I'm happy to have done. It's all in a lifetime.

So, if you're not in your winter yet… let me remind you, that it will be here faster than you think. So, whatever you would like to accomplish in your life, please do it quickly!

Don't put things off too long! Life goes by quickly. Do what you can today, as you can never be sure whether this is your winter or not!

You have no promise that you will see all the seasons of your life... so, live for today and say all the things that you want your loved ones to hear and remember... and hope that they appreciate and love you for all the things that you have done for them in all the years past!

(Ellipses in original)

# 1

## *My Story*

*J* *ust the ramblings of an old country boy from my heart to your heart, hoping you can relate and be able to say, "Yes, I understand. Been there!"*

This story I will be telling you came about on February 16, 2021. This was a day I shall never forget for I had a very unusual encounter with a man and a woman whom I believe to be angels. I believe this because of two important things that took place: the intense feeling of love and their disappearance. This is the incident that changed my life forever.

I had been walking at our local Cherokee Dam each day for more than a year. On this day, I had walked from the parking lot to the dam, half a mile away. There is a stairway at the dam, and as usual I went down the steps to the bottom of the dam for a better workout. The dam's height is 175 feet or equivalent to that of a 15-story building. When I got to the bottom and turned, I looked up and saw a man and woman standing on the top landing looking down at me.

There are four landing or rest areas on the stairway. At the first one, I stopped to rest. Looking up again, I noticed they were still standing there looking at me. After a short rest, I climbed on up to the second landing; they were there yet again. Now, I suppose, they might be waiting to inquire about my car. God had blessed me to be able to buy a Tesla, an all-electric car, in 2020, which was important to me. I had asked God to bless me with the ability to get one, and He did. For God had said, "Delight yourself also in the Lord, And He shall give you the desires of your heart." (Psalm 37:4 NKJV).

On several previous occasions after I parked at the dam, many people had asked about the car. It had become a means of opening a dialogue with people.

When I climbed to the third landing, I looked up. I didn't see them and supposed they had gone on their way. When I got to the landing where they had been standing, I found that they had just stepped back a few feet where they were out of sight until I was on the top landing.

I said, "Good morning," and to my surprise, the man said, "May we pray with you?" I had never had this happen to me before, but I said, "Yes, I would love that."

The next shocking surprise was when they walked over and put their arms around me in a three-way hug. Now this was at the pinnacle of the worldwide COVID-19 plague. No one was getting close to anyone not wearing a mask and none of us had masks.

I then felt a surge of love that I remembered from a dream I had back in the 1960s. I had seen Jesus and looked into His eyes with a feeling of love so great that I cannot find words to describe it. I can still feel that love, even today, when I think of that dream. At that point, I could not help myself. I blurted out, "Are you angels?"

The man began praying without answering me. He prayed, then she prayed. During each prayer I was so overwhelmed with a sensation of love that I didn't have words to express myself. I had a feeling of positive stimulation, a feeling of excitement like something big had happened. I was so overpowered by this feeling that my mind went blank. Later, as I thought back to the conversations, I was not able to remember what was said except for two messages: one was for my safety, and the other was that I would be able to do what I needed to do.

After a brief time, I said, "All right, see you later." I turned and went down a short ramp toward a fence that keeps people off the dam. It was about seventy-five feet. Then I turned the opposite way toward the parking lot, which was a half mile away. I was not out of sight for more than two minutes. The man and woman had started walking toward the parking lot, and I was expecting to see them ahead of me.

However, they had disappeared. I looked down the stairway just in case they had changed their mind, but nothing. They had just disappeared. From where I was, I should have been able to see them for a good fifteen minutes.

I asked God, "Were they your angels?" He didn't strike me blind for my doubting. However, I knew I had had a supernatural encounter of some kind. If they weren't angels, they would have to be magicians, for there is no way they could have gotten out of sight in such a short time.

I can't prove they were angels, but you can see the evidence by what you find in this book.

What baffled me was the woman. I couldn't remember a female angel in the Bible, but I did remember that Jesus said there is neither male nor female in heaven. As I was studying this, I remembered an incident from 2011. When I was going through a very bad health problem. I had a vision of a woman standing in front of me (more on this later). Then I found this passage in (Zechariah 5:9 NLT).

> Then I looked up and saw two women flying toward us, gliding on the wind. They had wings like a stork, and they picked up the basket and flew into the sky.

I have always believed the following scripture:

> Now faith is the substance of things hoped for, the evidence of things not seen. For by it the elders obtained a good testimony. By faith we understand that the worlds were framed by the word of God, so that the things which are seen were not made of things which are visible. (Hebrews 11:1–3 NKJV)

I believe that we always have angels with us, for the scriptures are clear about that.

> No evil shall conquer you;
> No plague will come near your home.
> For He shall order His angels to protect you
> wherever you go. They will hold you up with their

hands, so you won't even hurt your foot on a stone.
(Psalm 91:10–12 NLT)

This doesn't mean we won't have problems. In the Bible, we find many men and women who labored for God under problematic conditions.

As time went on, I kept remembering the part of the angels' message about what I needed to do. I couldn't think of anything that I needed to do. I began praying with more heartfelt passion, asking God, "What do you want me to do? What do I need to do?" I told Him, "I feel I am too old to do much of anything." After some days of praying, I began feeling His Holy Spirit moving in my life. The world began to seem brighter, and the feeling of excitement was like something had happened. I'm still rejoicing over this encounter to this day, thanking God for it.

You may be thinking, *why you? Why would God send an angel to you?* I asked myself the same question. Why me? What have I ever done to be worthy of this honor? I have spent a lot of time pondering this question. Why has God blessed me with all the miracles I have had in my life?

This was when a burning desire entered my heart to answer the call that filled my head with thoughts of my God. In my prayer each day, I asked, "What can I do?" Then one day, I heard a strong voice within my inner being say, *Witness.* I immediately asked, "How?" Over the next few days, I kept hearing the word *witness*, and I kept saying, "How?" I was bewildered. Why was I so troubled with the need to do something?

Then I began to feel His Holy Spirit moving on me, that feeling of boundless joy deep down in my heart. I began getting thoughts like, just tell them what I have done *for you.* I didn't remember all the things God had done for me, but it was only weeks later, as I continued praying, that things began coming back to me. Then I remembered what Jesus said:

> But the Helper, the Holy Spirit, whom the Father
> will send in My name, He will teach you all things,
> and bring to your remembrance all things that I said
> to you. (John 14:26 NKJV)

As I started writing these things down, increasingly, many more thoughts came to me. Then I thought, *why* not *me?* He had started working miracles early in my life. I began to understand that God had sent His angels to give me a mission to witness, to finish my life reaching out to others and showing them His love by my love.

But not knowing just how to get started on my new mission, I said, "I have heard You say *witness*, Lord, but how? In our culture today, it seems people don't want to talk about their faith or talk with strangers, especially about religion."

I heard again, *Witness!*

I asked again, "How, Lord? How can I accomplish this?"

After a few weeks of praying, He gave me the answer. He said to me, "You are Prince Albert. Go and witness."

I have been faithfully doing that for most of the time from that day to this day. I had not gotten the idea to write a book at that point; this came later.

Now, I don't believe it is my job to be critical of anyone. God said in (Romans 14:1 NLT).

"Accept other believers who are weak in faith, and don't argue with them about what they think is right or wrong."

Another passage, (Matthew 7:1-4 NLT) states:

> Do not judge others, and you will not be judged. For
> you will be treated as you treat others. The standard
> you use in judging is the standard by which you will
> be judged. And why worry about a speck in your
> friend's eye when you have a log in your own? How
> can you think of saying to your friend, let me help
> you get rid of that speck in your eye, when you can't
> see past the log in your own eye?

I am to love you and not love the things you do if I believe they are not godly. For I am representing Jesus. I am, therefore, to live the best life I can before you.

Because I am created in His image, I am to be a light to reflect His image so that you can see Him through me!

> You are the light of the world—like a city on a
> hilltop that cannot be hidden. (Matthew 5:14 NLT)

I understand most of us are a reflection of our home environments. We know only what we were taught by family and friends, what we hear and see, and what we know God has shown us. We are all on different levels of spiritual growth.

To advance our understanding about the kingdom of God is a personal choice. Do you know, or want to know, the meaning of your life? Do you want to know your loving Father God? Do you want to know what gifts God has waiting for you? Do you really want to go to heaven? If your answer is yes, follow this advice:

> Work hard so you can present yourself to God and
> receive his approval. Be a good worker, one who
> does not need to be ashamed and who correctly
> explains the word of truth. (2 Timothy 2:15 NLT)

The Bible is God's instruction book on how we can successfully negotiate the pitfalls of life.

He started His church and set it in order on the day of Pentecost, read Acts chapter 2. The Holy Spirit was given to teach people how to live a holy life and for the purpose of empowering His people to reach out to teach others how to live a life pleasing to Him.

Some people say you don't need to attend church to live for God. But I have learned that, because of the wickedness all around us, we need the camaraderie of other believers for encouragement and safety. We need the love of our fellow pilgrims, for the world will not give us love.

> And let us consider one another in order to stir up
> love and good works, not forsaking the assembling
> of ourselves together, as is the manner of some, but
> exhorting one another, and so much the more as you
> see the Day approaching. (Hebrews 10:24–25 NKJV)

I give thanks to my Lord and Savior Jesus Christ for saving my life, body, and soul despite my reckless, bad decisions in life. I will leave this world rejoicing and praising God for His great love for me and my loved ones.

My purpose in writing this book is to give witness to the miracles God has performed in my life and to give a public testimony of my repentance for my sins. It is my mission! God said, *"Witness."*

This is my witness; this is my story. By telling you what He has done and is doing for me, I hope that you can rejoice with me and that you may find your own story to become a witness. I believe each person has a story. Maybe you will write yours.

Jesus said in (John 14:13 NLT), "You can ask for anything in my name, and I will do it, so that the Son can bring glory to the Father."

These things that I describe herein are not unique or just for me. God has been doing these types of miracles for people all over the world from the day Jesus left to return to heaven to sit at His Father's right hand.

And even more and greater things are taking place daily. Look around you. You will find story after story about angels and Jesus appearing to people—not just to Christians, but to nonbelievers as well. You can find reports of people who have seen angels and had visions of angels, as well as of people who have seen Jesus in dreams and visions. There are testimonies of people having near-death incidents in which they have died for a short time and report having gone to heaven, or near heaven, or even hell.

I am fully convinced we are always surrounded by angels. God sends angels to us when He has something special, He want us to do. He sends them to us in dreams and allows us to have visions of them.

Angels speak to us from heaven; we can hear their voices within our very being. When I say, "from heaven," I'm not talking about a place far out in the universe, for I believe heaven is near, just on the other side of an invisible curtain.

The wind is also invisible. Some make the mistake of believing they see the wind. But they are not seeing the wind itself; they are seeing and feeling evidence of the wind. More on this later.

Speaking of angels. A 2011 poll by the Associated Press GfK revealed that 77 percent of adults believe these ethereal beings are real. Belief, the poll stated, is primarily tied to religion, with 88 percent of Christians, 95 percent of evangelical Christians and 94 percent of those who attend weekly religious services of any sort saying they believe in angels.[1] But belief in angels is fairly widespread even among the less religious. A majority of non-Christians think angels exist, as do more than 4 in 10 of those who never attend religious services.

Yet when someone talks about seeing an angel, some people are skeptical, even rolling their eyes.

It doesn't make any difference. I have met and talked to people who have told me they have had an encounter with one or more angels. I believe others have met angels without knowing it.

Many people also have stories about visions of Jesus. Some describe conversions similar to that of the apostle Paul.

One story that touched my heart was from a Jewish woman saying that Jesus had appeared to her and healed her of cancer. She is now a believer in Jesus Christ.

Missionary John Patton and his wife lived in the South Pacific, and he tells the story of wild natives who surrounded his home, threatening to kill them both. He said there was no way out, so they knelt and prayed, asking God to save them. They were ready and waiting for certain death. After some time, all the natives left.

Fast forward one year—through the grace of God, one of the

---

[1] "Poll: Nearly 8 in 10 Americans believe in angles," cbnnews. com, accessed February 21, 2024, https://www.cbsnews.com/news/ poll -nearly-8-in-10-americans-believe-in-angels/

chiefs of the tribe was saved, and the topic arose of that night when they had come to kill the missionary. John asked, "Why didn't you kill us?" The chief said, "Well, you had all those men surrounding you." John told him no men were there, only he and his wife.

The chief replied that he had seen hundreds of men with swords around the house. This is not the first time God had done that. Read 2 Kings 6:17.

You can find stories of people from all over the world turning to God because His Holy Spirit is touching the hearts of people with His great love. His love is the most powerful force on this earth.

Check out the podcast called "Everyday Miracles" by Julie Hedenborg and one by Sid Roth called "It's Supernatural." You will find many, many such stories.

It is happening more often now than at any time in history because God is making a final search for those who have a heart to turn to Him so that they may become witnesses for Jesus Christ.

I know there are many scoffers and mockers in this world, and that is their loss. Their doubt doesn't take away the reality of the existence of angels. Later in this book, I give witness of meeting what I came to believe was an angel back in the 1960s.

> Keep on loving each other as brothers and sisters. Don't forget to show hospitality to strangers, for some who have done this have entertained angels without realizing it! (Hebrews 13:1–2 NLT)

Think about that. Can you remember meeting someone who was very likable and enjoyable to talk with yet strange in some way that you couldn't forget for a long time?

> Therefore, angels are only servants—spirits sent to care for people who will inherit salvation. (Hebrews 1:14 NLT)

Don't be intimidated by an unbeliever or someone who mocks

or doubts you. Even some Christians will doubt you. Just tell what you have experienced in your life; that is your story, your witness.

Look, you mocker, be amazed and die! For I am doing something in your own day, something you wouldn't believe even if someone told you about it. (Acts 13:41 NLT)

When God knows there are no more hearts to win, that will be the day He will call in His army of workers and declare the end of the age, and the trumpet will sound.

> This is how it will be at the end of the age. The angels will come and separate the wicked from the righteous. (Matthew 13:49 NLT)

God knows there are many yet who will listen and come to Him. That is why He wants us, His children, to tell what He shows us.

In my eighty-nine years of life, I have had many strange and wonderful things happen to me and around me—some good, some not so good.

Most people make bad decisions at some time in their lives for none of us is perfect. I am one of them.

At one time, God called King David a "man after my own heart." Read Acts 13:21–23. Yet David had committed adultery with Bathsheba and had ordered her husband to be sent out in a battle so he would be killed.

> Then David confessed to Nathan, "I have sinned against the Lord." Nathan replied, "Yes, but the Lord has forgiven you, and you won't die for this sin." (2 Samuel 12:13 NLT)

I met a man who had been in prison for murder. He repented, and God called him to preach the good news, the Gospel, and witness about God's great love and forgiveness. You may ask, what was his sermon about? It was about what God had done for him and what he was doing for Him day by day. That's what witnessing is all about—telling others what Jesus has done for you and will do for them.

God also made it possible for him to be released from prison. He is now preaching God's good news to any who will listen.

A few years ago, I heard a story entitled "From the Mafia to the Ministry" told by a man who had been a hit man for the Mafia. He got caught, was put in prison, he converted to Christianity, started a prison ministry, and eventually was freed from prison.

I'm sure that, if you had known him before his conversion, you would have said it would be impossible for a mean killer to become a Christian. But God makes the impossible possible.

(Luke 7:47 NLT) "I tell you, her sins—and they are many—have been forgiven, so she has shown me much love. But a person who is forgiven little shows only little love."

It seems those that have great sins, have a greater appreciation for their forgiveness, than those that feel they have done nothing wrong. Some of these people will say I am a good person, why do I need to repent?

Because God said in (Romans 3:23 NLT)

"For everyone has sinned; we all fall short of God's glorious standard." I have failed God time after time and have learned some valuable lessons. One is that God will never leave you when you fail Him by making these bad decisions. The stories above point to that fact.

If we repent and ask God's forgiveness, there is nothing we can't do. We can do the seemingly impossible. All we need is faith and motivation.

We are His children; He doesn't expect us to be perfect yet, but if we strive for perfection, we will get there one day.

> Therefore, leaving the discussion of the elementary
> principles of Christ, let us go on to perfection, not
> laying again the foundation of repentance from dead
> works and of faith toward God, of the doctrine of
> baptisms, of laying on of hands, of the resurrection

of the dead, and of eternal judgment. And this we
will do if God permits. (Hebrews 6:1–3 NKJV)

We have a learning period from birth to death. When we were
born into the kingdom of God by faith in Jesus Christ, we entered
a new world, a spirit world. We are like babies, and our learning is
just beginning.

As newborn babes, desire the pure milk of the word,
that you may grow thereby. (1 Peter 2:2 NKJV)

Because we are adults in the earthly realm doesn't mean we are
adults in spiritual affairs. As I see it, we have one great problem.
Read the scriptures about the early days of the disciples. From that
day on, some people repented, and in their zeal and excitement, get
the idea they should start preaching before they are established in
the faith. Witnessing, yes. Telling why they are excited, yes. Trying
to lead others without knowledge, no.

As newly repented babies in Christ, we need to be mentored
by those who have been approved by God and then sent by God
to preach and teach. If you feel God has called you to preach, then
follow your heart and the guidance from the Bible.

Be diligent to present yourself approved to God, a
worker who does not need to be ashamed, rightly
dividing the word of truth. (2 Timothy 2:15 NKJV)

Some, before they have studied and prayed enough, fall under
the influence of Satan. He gives them delusions and half-truths, and
they think they have discovered some new truth that God gave only
to them. Some become false teachers and lead many astray because
they think they have learned a truth that everyone else missed. So
they go out preaching this new thing. Look what God said about that:

Let God's curse fall on anyone, including us or even
an angel from heaven, who preaches a different kind

of Good News than the one we preached to you. (Galatians 1:8 NLT)

I want you to understand that, if you happen to have gotten into one of these churches that has false teachers and become a new believer, you are saved because God can use them for His good.

But what God expects you to do is pray for understanding and study the Holy Bible, so you won't be deceived. His words are your road map to heaven. God will reveal to you the truth.

And you will know the truth, and the truth will set you free. (John 8:32 NLT)

Now search all of history, from the time God created people on the earth until now, and search from one end of the heavens to the other. Has anything as great as this ever been seen or heard before? (Deuteronomy 4:32 NLT)

Another great lesson I have learned in life is that you must be careful and watch out for those who preach good-sounding words that tickle the ear. They try to convince you that they are the only ones who have the truth.

I have had preachers come to me and say, "God told me to tell you…" and then proceed to try to indoctrinate me into believing their denomination is the only way to heaven, that they are the true church, or, as often happens, that I should join them in creating their new church based on a doctrine they think they have discovered.

It is estimated that 4,200 different religions exist in the world. Only God knows how many false teachers there are. Many men and women have a silver tongue, the ability of a slick, fast-talking salesperson. The only hope we have of finding the truth is by studying God's words and praying for His divine Holy Spirit to guide us into all truth.

I believe a great number of people are hungry for the love of

God, and the devil is watching for the poor soul who doesn't pray and study God's word. That soul could fall prey to the evil one.

I am not arguing for or against any group or denomination. My point is that we need to study God's word while praying for His understanding, and with faith. He will not let us go astray.

I learned that if we trust God, He will lead us by confirming what we hear and see by His word and by the Holy Spirit that dwells within us.

> He is the Holy Spirit, who leads into all truth. The world cannot receive him, because it isn't looking for him and doesn't recognize him. But you know him, because he lives with you now and later will be in you. (John 14:17 NLT)

Now is later! That is why we are told to study the Bible, His word. He said in (Joshua 1:8 NLT),

> Study this Book of Instruction continually. Meditate on it day and night so you will be sure to obey everything written in it. Only then will you prosper and succeed in all you do.

Only through Jesus Christ is there Salvation!

> I am the way, the truth, and the life. No one can come to the Father except through me. (John 14:6 NLT)

The only thing that can be new is the way the gospel is delivered. If only the men and women who claim to be preachers of the gospel would preach what God laid out by Jesus and His disciples to preach:

> "The time promised by God has come at last!" he announced. "The Kingdom of God is near! Repent of your sins and believe the Good News!" (Mark 1:15 NLT)

This is what the First Disciples taught:

**"Repent and believe on the Lord, Jesus Christ, and be baptized for the remission of sins."** This is the *good news*! That is the gospel story as it was then and is today.

> Jesus Christ is the same yesterday, today, and forever.
> (Hebrews 13:8 NLT)

If people would stop trying so hard to make church members and instead concentrate on making good disciples, the church that was born on the day of Pentecost would be much greater than it is now. There would be less confusion, and they could bring more people into the kingdom of God. Many false teachers have caused people to give up on trying to serve God. I have met many people who have related to me their bitter stories of sorrowful experiences in a church. I grieve for those who have had that kind of experience.

Later I will tell you my story of such an incident that nearly destroyed me. But God didn't forget me. He came to my rescue when I was down and nearly out. When I cried out to Him for help, He was there. Oh, how I love Him for His love is so great for me.

We need to teach people how to repent. Like with our earthly fathers, when we do something wrong, we understand he is displeased with us. We go to him and say, "Daddy, I am sorry." All loving fathers will say, "That's all right. I know you are sorry for what you did." And he will forgive.

So, it is with our heavenly Father when we understand we have made a mistake. We simply say, "Father, forgive me for I have sinned," and then believe in your heart that He has forgiven you for He said He would, and God can't lie. Then it will be as though it never happened; it's forgotten, never to be remembered by Him again.

Then we must learn to forgive ourselves, which sometimes becomes a hard thing to do. I know from my own experience that the human conscience can give us a bad time. Read Romans 8:1.

I have talked with many people who have said, "God won't save me because of my bad sins." Of course, these thoughts are coming from the evil one. But we have taken another step toward maturity when we learn that lesson.

All praise and glory to Jesus Christ in my sixty-some years of struggle to live a life pleasing to God and to be a soldier in the army of Christ. I have had many ups and downs.

Another lesson learned is that God will never give up on me or you. When I was about twenty-six years old, I heard God calling me. I answered, repented, and was born again by faith in His Son Jesus, and I became a son in the kingdom of God.

I was baptized as commanded by Jesus.

> Jesus came and told his disciples, "I have been given all authority in heaven and on earth. Therefore, go and make disciples of all the nations, baptizing them in the name of the Father and the Son and the Holy Spirit. Teach these new disciples to obey all the commands I have given you. And be sure of this: I am with you always, even to the end of the age. (Matthew 28:18–20 NLT)

We are born once in the flesh to die in this sinful world and born again in the Spirit into the kingdom of God, never to die. Born twice, die once.

I am so thankful for the peace in my heart. I am ready to go meet Jesus any time He is ready for me. When I lay down this earthly body and move into heaven in my new body to never die again. What a joyous day that will be! Friend, what God has done for me, He will do for you. Trust Him with all your heart. When in need, call on Him and believe by faith it is done. It's all about *faith*!

# 2 · The Good Life

Through it all, God has given me a wonderful family with great love for God our Father, Jesus our Savior, Holy Ghost our comforter, and one another.

God has rewarded me with four sons, two daughters, and many grandchildren, great-grandchildren, and great-great-grandchildren. I have brothers and sisters and a multitude of other beloved family members.

My family is so extensive that I have never met some of them. I expect to meet them in heaven, and we will be able to rejoice forever throughout eternity.

But this is not about me; this is about telling you what God has done for me and what He will do for you as an obedient, born-again son or daughter of God. This is only possible through faith in Jesus Christ.

He, Jesus, is the key that opens the door to the power of God. The two important things we need are *faith* and *motivation*. Faith is the first and most important thing, for without faith, there is no hope. The second is motivation, for without motivation, we don't even try. Nothing is impossible for you if you have faith and are motivated.

In the Bible story about the rich young man, we read,

Jesus looked at them intently and said, "Humanly speaking, it is impossible. But with God, everything is possible." (Matthew 19:26 NLT)

Now, it's not about what you or I have done. It's about what we can do starting today!

Yesterday is gone; today is the beginning of the rest of our lives. Will you ask God to wipe your record clean? Will you start your life over again by becoming a repentant-ed and forgiven, born-again child of God?

Jesus said in (John 14:13 NLT), "You can ask for anything in my name, and I will do it, so that the Son can bring glory to the Father."

Another purpose in writing this book is to tell you how you can get into this kingdom that offers eternal life. If you don't know, read on.

Some have said, "I can't believe in a God I can't see or feel." They say that only because they have not taken the time to search it out for themselves.

> You search the Scriptures, for in them you think you
> have eternal life; and these are they which testify of
> Me. But you are not willing to come to Me that you
> may have life. (John 5:39–40 NIV)

Many smart men and women have tried to prove there is no God, only to prove to themselves that there is! Scientists tell us we live in a three-dimensional world. Thereby, we can see people and objects clearly. We cannot doubt what we see in front of us. We know it is real!

Next, we know some things that are just as real can't be seen, and we believe in them because we can see the evidence.

Scientists will tell us that, according to superstring theory, there are at least ten dimensions in the universe. I boldly claim that the kingdom of God is in a dimension of its own.

I only want to point out there are invisible dimensions. We can see the first three dimensions. Number one is just a flat line; it can be any length.

The second dimension is a triangle or square that is flat. For example, a flat picture put in a frame becomes a three-dimensional image.

The next seven or so dimensions are where most people lose it. Consider some of the other dimensions that I know you will agree exist even though they are all invisible. They have been there from the beginning of time. I can't tell you what dimension number the following are in, but I can assure you that these things are beyond the third dimension.

Wind, heat, electricity, and radio waves are all invisible to our eyes, yet we know they are real. They are in an energy dimension. I don't think anyone has doubts about this unseen reality. You cannot see these things, but you can feel and see the evidence of them. No doubters here, right?

Wind is invisible, but you can see and feel the evidence of it. Feel the gentle breeze and see the destruction of strong storm winds. The fact that you can see the evidence of things that are invisible in the above dimensions proves that you do believe in things that you can't see. Why can't you believe the possibility of a God in another dimension or even a parallel universe?

Read what is said in (Psalm 119:2 NLT): Joyful are those who obey his laws and search for him with all their hearts.

From the beginning of time, God created this Earth and everything in it and on it.

> Then God said, "Let us make human beings in our image, to be like us." (Genesis 1:26a NLT)

> Then the LORD God planted a garden in Eden in the east, and there he placed the man he had made. (Genesis 2:8 NLT)

Even the angels have free will for there was an insurrection in heaven led by an angel called Satan who went to war with God. One-third of God's angels made the decision to go with Satan when he and his angels went down to the earth.

Satan corrupted Adam and Eve by telling them that God had lied and that they wouldn't die. They believed Satan and desired the forbidden fruit. So, they disobeyed God, and He set a curse on them.

The curse was that they lost paradise, and so all their descendants coming into this world after the curse are subject to it. However, God doesn't hold young children accountable until they understand the difference between right and wrong.

From that day on, when each person reaches a certain age and learns the difference between good and evil, they must decide who they want to follow. God created humankind with free will and the ability to choose between good and evil. That's why He gave us all a conscience.

When we do something wrong, our conscience will trouble us unless we have ignored it so much that we are hardened to it. You no doubt know what I am saying.

The first time you do something that you know is wrong, you feel guilty. If you ignore it, then you feel less guilty the next time, and after a while you stop feeling guilty at all. This is when you have become a hardened sinner.

After the disobedience of some angels, a war began between God and Satan. We, the created beings in the image of God, must choose who we want to follow.

Now, on this earth, God has allowed Satan to have some dominance over the earth for a time. God has set a time when He will destroy this earth and Satan and his followers will be cast into hell.

> Then I saw an angel coming down from heaven, having the key to the bottomless pit and a great chain in his hand. He laid hold of the dragon, that serpent of old, who is *the* Devil and Satan, and bound him for a thousand years; and he cast him into the bottomless pit, and shut him up, and set a seal on him, so that he should deceive the nations no more till the thousand years were finished. But after these things he must be released for a little while. (Revelation 20:1–3 NKJ)

> Now I saw a new heaven and a new earth, for the first heaven and the first earth had passed away. Also, there was no more sea. (Revelation 21:1 NKJ)

While God is creating this new heaven and new earth, we, His beloved people who made the choice to follow God, will be feasting in heaven. After that, we will be placed on this new earth to live as a ruling class of people. We will be perfected, with no more sickness, sorrow, or pain.

Make your decision. Making no decision is deciding to stay under the rule of Satan. Millions of people say, "I'm not going to follow this unseen God." That is why so many make gods out of earthly things like carved statues, gold, silver, or a multitude of other things they can see. Sorry, but one day they will have great regrets.

Let me explain it this way. To see God, open your mind to the possibility. Look at the multitude of believers. Can you honestly say all those people aren't intelligent enough to know the reality of a life after death? These people don't need to put their fingers in an electrical box to believe in a power that can't be seen.

Believers see, feel, and hear God. You can as well by seeing His works through tens of thousands of people coming into His kingdom daily, weekly, and monthly, people from all walks of life—Jews, Muslims, red, black, brown, and white. Some come by seeing Jesus in dreams or visions, some by having near-death experiences, and some by the witnessing of sincere, loving Christians.

God knows your every thought, and if you are just stalling but have a good heart, God may just send you an angel or give you a vision. You may think, I will give my life to God if He sends me an angel. But I ask, "What if you don't recognize the angel?" You may have missed your chance. Ask instead to see His people.

# 3

## My Start in Life and Family Tree

T his story is about what God has done and is doing. My public presentation is about His working with one of his creations—me. My start in life occurred when God brought a young man and a young woman together in marriage. He was nineteen, and she was fourteen. God created in the womb of the girl what would soon become a copy of the young man, a boy body. At the appointed time, God sent a spirit to live in that body, and when I breathed the breath of life, I became a living soul. Thereby, my spirit and body were joined together.

Every person in this world came the same way. We all started out equal. God created each person to walk a different path in life with a special purpose for each. He also gave us free will so that, at some point in life, we would learn about Him, Jehovah God, and learn that He wants us to walk our special paths in life for Him.

We learned that there is good and evil, and we learned about an enemy by the name of Satan and a loving God. We learned that we will have to choose whom we want to follow.

Satan has offered us grand lives full of fun and pleasure with no consequences for our sins, but that will never materialize. In the end we will find that it was a deception.

God offers us a short life here with many challenges, but an eternal life full of love and joy for those who endure to the end. We all are tempted by the enemy of our souls.

Jesus was not exempted from this temptation.

> Next the devil took him to the peak of a very high mountain and showed him all the kingdoms of the world and their glory. "I will give it all to you,"

he said, "if you will kneel down and worship me."
(Matthew 4:8 NLT)

Some of us try this kind of life for a season and then choose to follow God. Some never learn, and in the end, they find it was all an illusion leading to death here on earth and eternal life in a place called hell.

...The highway to hell is broad, and its gate is wide
for the many who choose that way. (Matthew
7:13 NLT)

Some of us learn about this loving God, and what He is offering us is eternal life in a place called Heaven. We also learn that if we choose to follow Him, we will have a season of challenges and trials to perfect our faith. Satan doesn't want to lose us. But God has promised us times of joy in this life as well as eternal life if we endure to the end.

Now all glory to God, who is able to keep you from
falling away and will bring you with great joy into
his glorious presence without a single fault. (Jude
1:24 NLT)

Most of what I learned came from Mom and Dad, later in life. My dad, Myron Elvis Williams, was born in 1913, the youngest of four children of Albert A. and Molly (Russell) Williams. His siblings were Milton, Johnny, and David; they and my dad are all now deceased.

My paternal granddad, Albert A. Williams, died before my dad was born, or shortly thereafter, while my paternal grandmother, Molly (Russell) Williams, died in the early 1950s.

My mother, Mable (Foreman) Williams, was born in 1918 in Arkansas. She was the oldest child of seven born to Alex and Sarah "Doll" (Masters) Foreman. Her siblings were George, Floyd,

Mary, Eve-may, Frances, and Earnest. Granddad Foreman was a landowner-farmer in Arkansas. (More on landowners later.) Grandmother "Doll" (Masters) Foreman was born around 1888 to an unknown-to-me, father and my great-grandmother, Sarah Jane Masters, who lived in or near Paragould, Arkansas, all of her 106 years.

Myron and Mable married in 1933 and raised nine children: Albert Lee, Elvis Junior, James Edward, twins Earlene and Alien, Alvin Ray, Mary Joyce, Wanda Faye, and Brenda. I was born near Manila, Arkansas, in an old log cabin out in the country.

My life and the lives of my entire family were filled with great struggles to survive poverty and difficulties! Through it all, it later became clear that God and His angels were sustaining, rescusing, and guiding us.

Mom was at the ripe old age of fifteen years and one month at my birth. She told me that, a few days after I was born, she had put me in the middle of the bed and went outside for a short time. When she came back in, she saw a big black snake on the bed with me. She let out a scream, ran over, picked me up, and ran outside, where she got the attention of some workmen in a field nearby who came running over and killed the snake.

In 1937, my brother Elvis was born, and at that time, there was a great flood. Mom said they had to wade through water for some miles to get to dry land, with Mom carrying baby Elvis. When they finally got to the first house not affected by the flood. A large dog attacked my dad while he had me in his arms. It's no wonder I have always been afraid of snakes and big dogs.

# 4     *My Early Life*

The first thing I can clearly remember occurred when my brother James was born in 1939. I was four-and-a-half years old. The following is to show the mercy of the almighty God. In the coming winter, we almost starved to death, but God came to the rescue.

Dad would go out in the cornfields looking for ears of corn that the farmer had missed when gathering in his crop. Now, the gathering of corn was done by hand in those days, so there wasn't a lot of corn to find.

Dad had to walk carrying the sack of corn he had to a mill, where they would grind the corn. The mill got half of it as a price for grinding.

One time when Dad went to the mill, he was waiting for his grain to be ground and someone offered to buy him a drink. You can guess the rest of that story.

Yes, he came home drunk—the only time I saw him drunk. I couldn't forget because we had a good-sized ditch in front of the house with a log to walk across when the ditch was full of water. This was one of those times for it had rained that day. Dad got about halfway across and fell into the water. Mom and I had a good laugh.

Dad also built rabbit traps, so we occasionally had fried rabbits and rabbit stew. After some time, Dad couldn't find more corn or rabbits because a lot of other people were doing the same thing he was doing too. So we were without food for a short time.

Dad went to the grocery store and asked for credit so he could get some food to hold us over until spring planting, when he could get a job. The only problem was that the store owner was helping a lot of families that were living on credit. He said he could not extend any more credit.

Then Dad went to some of the farmers, asking for any kind of work and telling them how desperate we were without food of any kind. Sometimes a farmer would send Dad home with a few food items. All three of us children spent time crying because we were so hungry.

God came to our recuse by touching the heart of a good man. One afternoon an old Model A Ford truck pulled up to the house. It was the local store owner with a load of food that would sustain us through the rest of the winter. Dad and Mom broke down crying as they thanked the man, and of course, all of us kids were crying. Even now, it brings tears to my eyes as I remember this tough time in our lives. Thank God that was the only time we ever came so near to starvation. This was winter 1939.

From that point on, Mom started going to church and gave her heart to God. I didn't know what was happening at that time, but I remember that Mom was different. She was calmer and more loving. She would give me more hugs and tell me she loved me more often.

When I think back to those days, one incident stands out to me. We were outside on a hot day. Mom was lying on a quilt in the shade of a tree when she took her lipstick out and said, "I don't need this anymore." I learned later why she did this. It was because she had dedicated her life to God, and the people of her church did not wear makeup, so she threw the lipstick away.

I went out, found it, and gave it back to her. She threw it away again. I thought it was a game, so I found it again. This time, she got up, walked over by the road, and threw it across the road into the weeds. I was never able to find it again, but I had a lot of fun hunting for it.

Later, I understood that this was when she had given her heart to God. I now had a praying mother, and from that day on, she never failed to tell me from time to time that she was praying for me.

In 1943, some months after Earlene and Alien were born, Alien died. And I think that was the time Dad gave his heart to God. Now I had both Mom and Dad praying for me.

Thinking back over the years, and all the things that I got myself into, I know those prayers are why I am still among the living.

I started school just before the age of seven in Manila, Arkansas. It was a late start by today's standards, but that was normal for most farm kids in those days. That is when I learned kids can be cruel, by taunting me with a phrase "Prince Albert in a can". Prince Albert tobacco was sold in a can in those days. I hated being called that at that time, but later when I learned what a prince was, I loved it. I have been called Prince Albert by some of my friends ever since. When people ask me my name, most times I say, "My friends call me Prince Albert."

Being the oldest child on a farm, I needed to help with chores more and more often. In the spring, I had to quit school early to help get the fields planted, and in the fall, I needed to help get the harvest done before winter set in. I could not start school until a month or more after it started.

# 5

## Our Move North

The only time I can remember ever getting in a full school year was in 1946–1948. We had moved from the farm in Missouri to Berrien Springs, Michigan.

This had come about when one of Dad's cousins came down south to visit his mother and my dad. He told Dad he might be able to get him a job at Clark Equipment Company in Berrien Springs, where he was working. Dad followed him back and got the job.

The rest of the family continued living in a landowner's shack in Missouri. Dad worked for a time and then came back for us when the landowner found out that Dad had moved to Michigan. He told him to get his family out of his house. We had nowhere else to go.

Dad piled all seven of us into a Model A Ford, and I do mean piled. He tied boxes of our clothing and a few other odds and ends on top of the car, on the back bumper, and on the front fenders. Later in life when I saw *The Beverly Hillbillies*, I was able to relate.

Dad's top speed was about thirty-five miles per hour. If I remember right, it took three days to get to Michigan. We would park and camp alongside the road at night. The three smaller kids would sleep in the car, while Mom, Dad, Elvis, and I would sleep out on the ground.

When we got to Michigan, Dad didn't have money to rent a house, so we stayed a few weeks at his cousin's house. Now picture this: Dad's cousin Bill, his wife, and their four kids lived in a house that was too small for them, then we added seven more. You get the picture.

Dad couldn't find a house to rent for no one wanted to rent their house to a hillbilly family with five kids. Then one of the guys Dad was working with in the shop told him he had an old chicken house. If we wanted to use it, he would give it to us at no cost.

Dad went out to look it over and decided he had no choice but to take it. This place was about two and a half miles outside of Berrien Springs, but Dad and Mom were desperate to get out of his cousin's house and his cousin just as desperate to get us out.

Anyway, Dad loaded all of us and our belongings into the car on a Saturday morning, and we moved to the chicken house. It still had chicken droppings on the floor. The walls were bare; we lined them with cardboard. It had one small window, one light bulb, and no plumbing. The toilet was an outhouse. Our water came from an outside water faucet at the main house.

We went to work, and by that night, we had it reasonably clean. As I recall, the farmer gave us straw to put on the floor for bedding, and somebody gave us some quilts and blankets. The farmer set an old wood stove in place and ran the smoke pipe out the window. This was now home sweet home.

I don't remember the size of the shack, but I would guess it to be about ten feet by twenty feet. Today it would be called a tiny house if it could be called a house at all.

This was sometime in August 1946, so it was summer, but the nights were cold. Later, we kids started going to school. Now this was an experience no one could forget.

From day one, we were made fun of and picked on by bullies. Looking back on it, I can understand why, but that doesn't take away the hurt. We were dressed in our best clothes, but they had patches on them and our shoes had holes in the soles.

One boy was my personal devil. He picked on me from the start of school until the day's end. The pencil sharpener was in the back of the room near my desk, so this boy would sharpen his pencil in order to walk by me and call me names like "dumb hillbilly trash" and so on. Sometimes, he would give me a slap on the back of my head.

Most of the kids in the class were nearly as tough on me, and no one wanted to be seen talking to me at recess. My brother Elvis had his own personal hell as well, but I don't remember my brother James talking about his life at school.

To this day, I have a piece of pencil lead in my leg where the bully jammed it in, as he walked by. When I cried out, the teacher wanted to know what was going on, so I told her he had jammed his pencil into my leg. He said he had tripped, and another boy sitting close by backed up his story.

Sometimes at recess, the bully and some of his friends would gather around me, call me names, slap my face, spit on me, and punch me. I would end up crying from frustration, but that makes it more fun for the bullies. I soon learned to just endure it. My time was coming.

One day this bully started on me after school while I was waiting for the bus, when most of his friends had gone home. I am sure he regretted that day for a very long time.

Now, my mom has taught me not to fight. She had told me about turning the other cheek. But this day I couldn't take any more. I flew into a rage, fists flying. I had him on the ground and was sitting on him, beating him, when a teacher pulled me off. This time *he* was crying, like a baby.

The bus arrived, so the teacher told me to go home and to come back the next day with a parent and report to the principal's office. Dad was working and couldn't get off, so Mom, Earl, and I had to walk to school with her carrying Alvin Ray.

The bully was there with his mother. The principal talked with both of us with our mothers, one at a time. I told the principal what had been going on from the time I had started school, crying most of the time. I want to believe he believed me and did what he could, for he talked very gently and kindly.

And as you can guess, the bully said I was lying, and for that, I was suspended for a few days. I also didn't get to go out for recess for some time—I don't remember how long. But I was very happy not to go out. I don't know if the bully got any kind of discipline. I feel sure he probably did.

Some months later, I caught the bully downtown by himself on a Saturday. I told him that if he ever picked on me again, I would catch him when he was alone and beat him to death. I think he believed me because, when I had him down in the schoolyard, I had shown him that I could beat him. And I was big for my age. I had no trouble from that day on.

Sometime near Christmas, another farmer about a mile on out from town said he had a two-bedroom house in a field behind his house that needed a lot of cleanup and repairs. The farmer made Dad a good deal. I'm not sure what it was, but I remember that Mom and Dad were very happy.

We lived there for two years, but then the company Dad worked for shut down and moved to Battle Creek, Michigan. He could have worked in the plant in Battle Creek, and he spent some time looking for a house in that area, but he couldn't find a place.

At that time, our family had five boys, Mom was about to give birth to my sister Mary. She was born just before we moved back to Missouri.

# 6

## Moved Back South

We moved to a rented house in Senath, Missouri, where Dad worked for different farmers wherever he could find someone that needed help. But it was not steady work.

I would go out after school with a gunny sack and pick up soda bottles to return them to the grocery store for two cents per bottle. Other kids did the same, so the pickings were slim. Sometimes on a Saturday I would make as much as twenty-four cents for my day of work. Most times, it was less.

When I turned sixteen, I quit school. By that time, I thought I knew all that I needed to know to work on the farm, or wherever I could find something to do. Boy, if only I could have seen the future.

But Dad had gone to school only through the second grade, and Mom had gone through the third or fourth. So they had no knowledge of the need for higher education, and I wasn't encouraged to go further. It was all about working from sunup to sundown.

I worked in the cotton fields from about the age of six, picking cotton with Mom and Dad. I started by picking and making piles of cotton in the middle of the row that Dad was in, moving ahead of him. As he got to the pile, he would scoop it up and put it in his cotton sack. This was a big help to him.

For picking cotton, people were paid by the pound, something along the lines of about $1.50 to $2.00 per hundred pounds. It was a big deal for one person to pick three hundred pounds in a day.

Mom could pick about one hundred pounds because she had to take time to care for the little ones. Most of the time, I had to stay with the babies. Mom had to breastfeed those who were under one year old.

She also did all of the diaper changing. At that time, there was no such thing as disposable diapers. I got the job of washing the diapers.

Our lunch meal was mostly peanut butter and crackers. Sometimes we ate beans and taters with cornbread if Mom had time to make them before we went back out to work.

Our family's average amount picked per day was about 350 pounds with my help. Some men could pick up to 300 pounds in a day by themselves if they worked late into the night. The farmers would not let pickers start too early in the morning if there was a lot of dew. He did not want to pay for wet cotton because he would be paying for water.

Most farmers paid cash at the end of the day. If we were able to pick three hundred or more pounds, we were *rich, rich*. The problem was that it was hard, backbreaking work.

I suffered a lot of back pain. Sometimes it would hurt so badly that I would be in tears. When I complained about it, Mom and Dad would tell me that everyone's back hurt. They had no idea that I had a birth defect. I was twenty-two years old before I found out why my back hurt so bad. I learned to suffer quietly and endure the pain.

There were always more people looking for work than there were jobs available. Sometimes after three or four days of picking, one farmer's field would be picked clean. Then Dad would find another farmer who needed help, if there was anyone nearby. So if we worked an average of three days a week, we were doing good.

There were a lot of people like us who were always searching for a way to get food. There was no welfare as we know it today. I do remember a government program that would allow people to get a small amount of food. However, it was not passed out in rural areas. Even if we could get to the bigger city where food was, we would have had to walk there and then carry it back home. Sometimes they would run out of stock before we got to the place of disbursement.

When we were unemployed, it didn't mean we had time off. Mom would grow a garden, wash all our clothes by hand, and cook our meals on a wood stove. My job was to keep the wood box filled, pump water by hand, and carry it where needed. I also kept water and food out for the chickens.

Dad would busy himself cutting wood for cooking and building up a supply for heating in the winter. With no power tools, it was a very big job. He had to work through the summer cutting and hauling wood home from the woods, and then we had to stack it, as we didn't have anything to haul it on. We carried a lot of it in our arms.

Before I was old enough to be of much real help— between the ages of eight and ten years old—Dad would make two or three trips to my one. Of course, all of us kids who were old enough to help were always kept busy doing what we could.

No, we didn't just volunteer. It was a big job for Mom and Dad to keep us doing our chores. Like any kids, we wanted to play, not work. But Mom and Dad knew that part of the Bible that says, "Spare the rod and spoil the child," and they obeyed that command. I thought God must surely be happy with them.

One time when I was about thirteen or fourteen, we were picking cotton in the fields. Well, cotton bolls are just the right size for throwing and great fun to use in a fight with other kids. Of course, it was not entirely safe. Kids could get hurt, especially the younger ones. And it was a waste of cotton. So we were told time and time again not to do that.

One day, some of us kids were way down at the far end of the field, away from our parents. Someone started a fight by throwing a cotton boll. Next thing you know, we were all having the time of our lives. I don't remember if Elvis was in our group, but he likely was.

Then there came a couple of dads. One was mine. He stopped to cut off a branch from a cotton stalk, and I knew I was in trouble. I said, "Dad, I'm not doing anything." He said, "I know. That's why I'm going to whip you—because you are supposed to be picking cotton."

Sometimes we would work many days cutting, splitting, and making piles of wood about a half mile from the house. If Dad could borrow the landowner's wagon to haul it up to the house, we would have it easy.

One winter, maybe in 1944, we cut wood to sell to help us buy food. This was a very hard time as well. Landowners were glad to give us access to the trees for free because they wanted to clear the woods out to make it into farmland. The requirement was that we had to clean up what we did not use by burning the excess limbs.

We would use a crosscut saw (that's a two-man saw—or one man and an eleven-year-old boy) to cut the trees down and then saw them into blocks about eighteen inches long. Then we split the blocks with a hand ax.

Dad wasn't able to borrow a wagon for this project, so he built a wooden sled and put a long handle on it so that he, Elvis, and I could pull it. We had to haul it up to a road about a half a mile away and stack it in ranks in the front yard. I believe the rank was a stack of eighteen-inch wood that was eight feet long and three feet high. We sold the wood for about five dollars per rank. Now that was a lot of hard labor for so little, but that was the going price.

Thank God we were living close to Grandma and Grandpa Foreman at that time. My grandma canned a lot of the garden vegetables. She would bring over some canned goods, or Mom would send Elvis and me to get them.

At that time, we did not have a car. As best I can remember, we got our first car in the fall of 1942 or 1943. We were living about ten miles outside of Marked Tree, Arkansas, so we either walked or hitched a ride when we needed to go to town.

Few cars were on the road in those days, for we weren't on a busy road. It was just an old dirt road, more like a lane. Sometimes, we would not see a car all day.

Most of the time, the old car we got wouldn't start. It didn't have a starter; we had to crank it by hand. So each time we wanted to go to town, one would have to crank and crank. Maybe it would start, and then maybe not.

Now, we had to be very careful when cranking because, sometimes, the car would backfire, spin the crank backward, and break an arm. Lots of arms were broken that way back in those days. It's very hard to work with a broken arm, and no one would hire someone who had one. If the person with the broken arm was the only one in the family who worked, the family would likely go hungry. So the best way to get the car started was to push it.

There was no blacktop on our road, just loose sand, and it's very hard to push a car on a flat sandy area. Mom and all of us kids would get behind the car and push. Dad would open the door and push it from outside. When we got it rolling good, he would jump in, put it in gear, then let out the clutch. Most of the time, it would start on the first try. Praise God.

# 7
## Landowners and Living on a Farm

In the spring of 1949, I got a job on a farm driving a tractor for forty cents per hour. This was a dream job; I just sat there and drove from one end of the field to the next. Then later that year, I got promoted to nighttime driving, and it paid fifty cents per hour. I was nearly fifteen, and I was on my way to making a man's living.

There were three kinds of farmers in those days. First, a landowner was the person who owned the land. We called those landowners the rich people. Some were very rich, some were just comfortable or middle-of-the-road rich, and some were just getting by. As always, some would lose their land after having a bad year—like too dry or too wet—especially if there were two bad years in a row. They would have to sell their farms if they didn't have enough money to plant a crop the following year or were too discouraged to keep trying.

The second kind of farmer was a renter, what we called middle class. This farmer rented farmland from a landowner at a certain amount per acre, and most had to pay the total year's rent upfront. Some landowners would wait until the end of the year to get their money, but the renter would have to pledge his equipment as collateral.

Land renters had to not only pay rent, but also have enough money to plant their own crops. In the early days, that meant they had to have horses or mules, plows, cultivators, a wagon, and other equipment, plus money to buy seeds and other supplies. They also needed to buy food to feed their families until they could gather in their crops in the fall. If these types of farmers had a bad year, many went broke and lost all of their equipment.

The third farmer was a sharecropper. These were the poor people, the lowest class of farmers. That was the class we were in, and it was just one step above being a slave. A sharecropper made a deal with a landowner to farm the land and give the landowner a share of the earnings. Each landowner would make up his own deal—take it or leave it. Some of them wouldn't keep their word, and they never put anything in writing.

Landowners would supply sharecroppers with a shack to live in and all the tools needed for the work. The sharecroppers paid for their seeds and did all the labor, including getting the crop harvested and to market.

Landowners would lend sharecroppers money to live on until the end of year and then split the crop money fifty-fifty. Any money the sharecroppers had borrowed had to be repaid from their shares.

Now, here is the rub. If it was a bad year, the sharecroppers' half of the money was not enough to pay back all their borrowed money. Then they were called debtors, and they weren't allowed to move until their debts were repaid. If they did move away, the landowners could have them put in jail.

The sharecropper lived in a house provided by the landowner. The landowner would require the sharecropper to do all kinds of work around the farm during the winter, like repairing tools, fixing fences, and cutting wood. For that work, the landowner would pay the worker what he wanted to—maybe just fifty cents per hour—and that was just enough to keep the sharecropper from starving to death.

Some landowners would tell sharecroppers a lot of things that weren't true and make promises that they didn't keep. It seemed that some landowners thought these people were just trash because they had nothing.

If sharecroppers had barely made it one year, most would look for a better deal for the next year. So we did a lot of moving. Usually we would stay one year, but sometimes we might stay two or three. We would stay longer than one year if we had made enough money to pay off our debt at the end of the year and still have enough to get us through the winter. If Dad liked the owner, we would stay another year.

We stayed with one farmer for two or three years because he was a good and kind man. This is the only man I remember by name: Hester Parker. He was what I would call a Christian.

He had a lot of land and thereby a lot of sharecroppers. He was good to all of his tenets and helped when they were having a bad time. He treated all kids well and always talked to us whenever we ran into him. We all loved him.

Each Saturday, most farmers went into town to shop or just to get away. As a kid of about eleven, the big deal for me was finding Mr. Parker while we were in town. It became a fun game because whenever we found him, he would give us kids five cents each.

In the summer, some businesses would put on free movies outside, projecting it on the side of a building. A lot of people could not afford to pay the ten cents to go to a theater.

Now, at the end of harvest, we had to buy food in bulk for the coming winter. Dad would buy a hundred-pound barrel of flour and hundred-pound sacks of great northern beans, rice, oatmeal, and sugar, as well as other food items in bulk.

Farmers would kill hogs in the fall, and Dad would help. For his labor the farmers would give him all the parts that they did not want, plus maybe ham and a side of bacon. Then Dad could buy more if he wanted to.

However, there were no deep freezers available. Only two ways existed to keep meat from rotting too quickly, and they were to smoke it, or keep it in salt. We had no means to smoke it.

The way to keep it in salt was by building a tray about two feet wide and as long as needed. Some places we went to already had such trays. We would lay down a bed of salt about one to two inches deep, place all the raw meat on this bed, and cover it with more salt. With the cold winters, it would remain edible up to April or May, sometimes a little longer.

Now if we were hard up enough when the meat was nearly rotted, we would boil it and make soups. I don't remember throwing any away, though I do remember having to scrape off maggots sometimes. But I learned that rotted meat will not harm people if it is boiled long enough.

Most people grew potatoes. To keep through the winter we would dig a big hole in the yard. Next we would put straw in the hole, then fill it with potatoes, turnips and apples if we could buy some. We would cover this with more straw and put dirt on top. Throughout the winter months, we would dig down to get out about what we would need for two weeks.

If we had made enough money, we would be able to buy some clothes and shoes. We always went barefoot from spring until fall so as not to wear our shoes out before the next in line could receive them as hand-me-downs. This is when being the oldest child should have paid off; I would need new clothes, while all my brothers wore my hand-me-downs.

I grew like a weed, so I always needed new clothes and shoes. Well, there is always something to mess up a good thing, Mom's youngest brother was one year older than me, so I started getting his hand-me-downs. It was not all bad. I was only the second one to wear them.

This is not to say we never got new things to wear. In the good years, we got new stuff. Sure wish they would have had Goodwill stores back then.

Elvis got my cast-offs, James got his, and down the line it went to our little brother, Alvin. In those days, when a pair of jeans got ripped or a hole in them, Mom would take out the needle and thread and patch them. By the time they got to Alvin, they kind of looked like Joseph's coat of many colors.

I don't remember ever seeing fat sharecropper farm kids. The only fat kids I saw were city kids.

Life was tough, but we had a lot of company. There were and always will be more poor people than rich and comfortable people. This was when I learned that, no matter how hard we had it, someone else was worse off than us. Some poor kids had drunken dads. Those were the kids who had it real hard. I remember seeing kids whose dads would beat them. Sometimes I would cry with them.

In 1950, I got my driver's license on my sixteenth birthday. All I had to do was walk into the driver's license office and ask for it. They asked me two questions: my birth date and whether I could drive.

That winter, I got my first real paying job on my own, a coal-delivery job. Most people in those days burned coal for heat and cooking. My job was to shovel coal onto an old 1940 Ford truck, haul it to where it was to be delivered, shovel it off, and then return and do it over again.

Some places had a coal chute window to put it into, but in most places, I had to put it in a small tub and carry it into the house. I was paid about thirty-five cents per hour.

When the company had a lot of orders (mostly at the start of winter), I would work ten hours or more a day, six days a week. I was in great pain at the end of each day. My back would have me in tears. But I thought I was a rich man, making $3.50 per day or more.

I had worked in the cotton fields chopping cotton from sunup to sundown for two dollars per day, whereas Dad would get three dollars. However, he had to help me keep up with all the other field workers. A field boss set the pace, and anyone who couldn't keep up was let go.

# 8

## My First Miracle

One day in 1951, before I went north, I was running around with one of my cousins. His dad had a nearly new four-door car. He let my cousin borrow it one Saturday night so we and another friend could go to a wrestling match about fifteen miles away.

We were running a little late, so my cousin was driving much too fast on a gravel road. We came to a place where a road came into the road we were on. The ditches on the sides of both roads had tall weeds, so we didn't see the kids on a bicycle until they crossed the road in front of us.

My cousin swerved to miss them and lost control when we hit the ditch on the right side of the road. The car went airborne and landed upside-down in the ditch on the opposite side of the road, pointing in the direction we had come from. We crawled out with only a few bruises.

The car was totaled. The front had crumpled up to the windshield, and the rear end was caved into the back of the front seats. The only place that was not damaged was where we three had been seated.

We later learned why we survived without injury or death. The same kid who had run across the road in front of us, along with his brothers, had dug a big hole in the ditch just a little way from their house so that when it rained, they had a swimming pool. The front passenger part of the car was in that hole and was the only part of the car that wasn't damaged. I didn't think to thank God, but I know that my mom and dad did, along with my cousin's parents.

I left home and moved to Rockford, Illinois, in the fall of 1952. I got a job working for the Singer Sewing Machine Company, where my starting pay was $1.10 per hour and I worked only forty hours per week.

I thought I was rich when I got my first check of forty-four dollars before taxes. Wowee! And it was the easiest work I had ever known. All I had to do was stand in one place and feed some small wood pieces into a sanding machine on a conveyor.

I was living with Dad's first cousin's daughter, the sister of the one with whom I had been in the wreck. I soon bought my first car for about a hundred dollars.

Of course, I would get homesick. So sometimes after work on Fridays, I would head for home in Missouri and get back in time for work on Monday morning, sometimes without going to bed first. I did this about once a month for a while. It was about 430 miles one way, and gasoline was ten to twelve cents per gallon.

I would work all day and then drive through the night to get home, where I would sleep for a few hours, get up, and run around all day and half of the night, showing off. Then I would go back to Illinois late Sunday afternoon. I didn't get much sleep, but I was young and could take it.

In 1953, I started dating for the first time, and then I met the most beautiful girl I had ever seen. Her name was Jane Anne Morrison. She was born in 1935 the daughter of Robert and Geraldine Morrison. Jane was the fourth of nine children.

I, Albert L. Williams, and Jane Anne Morrison were married on August 27, 1953, in Kennett, Missouri. Our first baby boy came in September of the next year.

# 9

## My Second and Third Miracles

I had gotten acquainted with a boy about my age in the shop where I worked. For some reason I can't recall his name—probably because we didn't have enough time together before he lost his life.

We ran around together on most weekends except when one of us was out of town. I was from Missouri, and he was from Arkansas.

Sometime around August 1954, this friend bought himself a new, hot Chevy Bel Air convertible. He was excited about it, and on our lunch break, he took me out to show it to me. Then he said, "I want you and Jane to go out with me Saturday night and celebrate with me." I told him that we would.

However, when I told Jane about it, she said, "You go ahead and go with him. I don't feel that good." She was eight months pregnant at that time.

I told her that maybe I shouldn't go, but she insisted that I should. Otherwise, our friend would be hurt.

The next day, I told my friend that Jane would not be going, but I would. As the week went on, I was troubled. Something was nagging at my mind or conscience. By Friday evening, I was feeling very miserable.

I met my friend out in the parking lot as we were going home. He said, "See you later." I almost said OK, but instead, I said, "I'll not be able to go. Sorry, but my wife needs me. She is not doing well." Immediately, I started feeling relief.

The next day, we got word that he, along with two other friends, was killed in a wreck. As I got the story, they were driving between another town and our hometown. (We had done the same thing before; there was a place we liked in another town).

According to the local newspaper, he had hit the back of a stalled semi-truck at about two o'clock in the morning. It was foggy, and he was doing about eighty miles per hour—I'm sure he was drunk.

It took me a while to get over that. I understood later that the nagging I felt had likely been from an angel of God. By this time, I was beginning to think about God. I was still a sinner, and I don't remember thanking God for saving my life.

When I next saw my mom, she gave me a sermon and pleaded with me to give my heart to God. I told her, "Later," like most rebellious children do.

Another miracle occurred in 1955. I bought a super cheap Harley-Davidson motorcycle. One day, while running down a city street, a car ran a red light in front of me. I didn't even have time to touch my brakes.

I hit the car in the middle of the back door and totaled my bike. I remember looking down at the top of the car as I went over it. I lost some skin and was badly bruised.

God's angels were on the job. There could have been another car in the other lane. Again, I didn't think to thank God.

About a year and a half later Jane's health went downhill, and she got terribly sick. By then, she was carrying our second boy. We named him Donnie Lynn. When he was born, we knew something was wrong from the start. The doctors told us that his brain hadn't developed, likely because Jane had been so sick the whole time she carried him.

Medical bills began to pile up as we had no insurance, and Donnie had to stay in the hospital for two more weeks. Then every two weeks afterward, Jane had to take him in to see the doctor for a checkup. He was not doing well.

After some time, the doctor asked us to take him to a clinic in Chicago to be checked by some experts. It was ninety miles away. We took him once a month for about a year.

We were barely able to get by as it was, and now we had the added expenses. I was working a full-time job that paid $1.35 per hour. I then found a part-time job pumping gas for $1 per hour.

At the end of the year, the doctors told us there was nothing more they could do, and that he would live only for a few years. As it turned out, he lived for seven years in total.

I was having a hard time, but Jane had it much harder than me. She was still trying to get over her sickness and caring for two infants. Then, in 1956, she had a miscarriage, most likely because of her sickness. Then she finally began to recover her health somewhat.

The following year, in 1957, we had another child whom we named Gary Wayne. Jane had recovered her health to a point, but wasn't in the best of health for many years. And now she had three children to care for while she was still somewhat weak.

We had no one who could come to help; everyone we knew was having it as hard as we were. I did all I could to help at home. I was working ten-hour days and taking all the extra hours I could get. This hardship was relentless. Week after week, the bills piled up. Each payday we faced the chore of trying to figure out which bills to pay.

We were really heartbroken, and somewhere in this time frame, we talked about needing God's help. But we did nothing about it at that time. As I remember, we couldn't decide what church to go to. Jane had been brought up Catholic, and I had been brought up Protestant.

We couldn't afford to rent an apartment and had been staying in Jane's parents' garage for more than a year. So in about 1957, we moved from Rockford, Illinois, to Michigan, where an uncle of mine owned an eighty-acre farm.

He was living and working in another state. He agreed to let us live there rent-free and to pay all the expenses for the house. In exchange, all I had to do was work as a caretaker on a farm, which included plowing the fields, planting and gathering the corn, and taking care of his hogs, feeding and watering them. He also purchased a cow, so we had milk for the kids. We were very grateful to him.

For the first year, I did odd jobs. Then I got a job as a laborer in a factory called Rudy Manufacturing Company in the fall of 1958. Things began to look brighter.

However, Jane was pregnant again, and she was still not in the best of health yet. Her doctor called me in for a private talk. He informed me that she might not survive having another baby and caring for Donnie as well. He said he had checked on an institution about forty miles away that would take care of Donnie at no cost to us.

When I told Jane this, she started crying. We both broke down and had a big crying spell. Finally, she agreed that she was too weak and exhausted to keep going on the way she was.

Reluctantly, we agreed to put Donnie into the care of the institution. It took part of the load off her, and she started getting a little better.

Then our next boy was born. We named him Stanley Scott. However, the money woes got worse.

We both wanted to see Donnie as often as possible. We started making the eighty-mile round trip on Saturdays and Wednesdays. We had to take our children with us, so we would take turns staying out in the car with them while the other went inside to visit Donnie.

I had to arrange to take a half day off on Wednesdays. I was so thankful that my boss was very understanding, but I kept worrying, afraid I would lose my job. It was supposed to be just a temporary summer job, anyway, and I was hoping to get some of my bills paid before winter came.

The trips were cutting into our money supply even more. Finally, we had to cut out the midweek trip. Jane took it hard, but she understood we just couldn't do it.

From the beginning, it was a very tough time for Robert, our firstborn. From the time that Donnie was born, Rob got very little attention from his mother or me for two very important reasons: she was very sick and caring for Robert, Donnie, Gary, and Stanley, I was working at every job I could find—most times working seven days a week. Looking back on it, I don't know how either of us did it. Only God could have made it possible.

Robert had to grow up faster than he should have had to. He helped his mother by holding Gary when she was caring for Donnie and holding Donnie when she was caring for Gary. His responsibility was never-ending. I don't remember him complaining, but I do remember Jane telling me she didn't know what she would do without him.

I worked two jobs seven days a week for more than a year. Then I became weak and sick. Our family doctor said that I was working myself to death. He told me that if I wanted to be around to help my family, I would have to stop what I was doing. Money problems multiplied again.

I got the little girl I wanted in May 1961. We named her Kathy Anne. We now had four boys and one girl. Then came Alberta Sue in September 1962; I now was blessed with two beautiful girls . About the middle of 1963, Donnie died. I will share more on this story later.

I met what I came to believe was an angel in the shop where I was working just after Donnie died. I can't remember how long it was after his death. As one would expect, it was very hard for all of us—but more so for Jane. Jane's grief was so great that she never recovered as the years went on.

Then our last child, Arlan Glenn, came in 1968. The other children all helped as they became old enough. By the time Kathy, Alberta, and Arlan were old enough to enjoy their mother, she was deep into a depression from which she never recovered. The children didn't get to see the loving mother she had been before Donnie passed.

Since Robert was the oldest, the hardship never stopped for him up to the day he left home. He has a godly love for his brothers and sisters as well as for me.

However, he grew up with a big handicap—me! I was not able to teach him how to express his love. Yes, he, like me, has made many bad decisions and mistakes, like a chip off the old block. But who hasn't? I know exactly how he feels for I believe I was mostly at fault.

Looking back from today, I can only wish I had spent more time loving him and telling him when I was so proud of him for the good things he had done. None of my other children had such a hard beginning in life as he.

I am so thankful for such a great loving heavenly Father and for

His forgiveness as we have learned to forgive one another. There is no one on this earth who has not made mistakes.

All of my children have a great love for me, though most of the time I feel unworthy of their love because I have failed them so many times. Yet I also know that I did the best I could for them. I was not endowed with a godly understanding of how to raise a family. I only knew what I had learned from my parents, and they did the best they knew how with me.

Most times, when I got home from work, I was tired to the bone. But all my children would run out to greet me, giving me hugs, kisses, and the love I needed to let me know it was worth the efforts I made and that I was a good dad.

One day when I got home, the boys came running out. As they pushed the storm door open, it swung back just as the youngest son put his hands out to push the swinging door. The glass broke, and he went through the opening. He fell onto a long, pointed piece of glass that punched into his chest over his heart.

We lived several miles out in the country, so it took some time to get to the emergency room. Once there, we had to wait for a doctor to come from home. The doctor stitched him up and sent us home with instructions as to how we were to treat the wound once we were home. To make matters even more stressful, we had left our oldest son, Robert, who was about nine years old, at the house with Gary and baby Kathy. God was with us, along with His angels for nothing more happened to us at that time.

As I think back now on the pleasure of coming home after a hard day at work, with Jane and all my children making me feel that I was very much loved and appreciated, I am brought to tears. I was always refreshed and ready to do it all over again the next day.

This is one of the reasons I feel such great love for them all—my understanding and acknowledging of what they missed and the hardships they endured. I didn't, however, understand what had happened to Jane after Donnie's death.

She seemed to have just given up on life. For the next twenty years, she just existed with no real life in her. She didn't want to do anything or go anywhere. She was alive, but dead inside, with no joy in her life. And she wouldn't talk to me about what she was thinking. She just told me to leave her alone, and I did because I was working long hours each day. From this point in my life, I can understand that I failed her in a big way.

We never had enough money to buy the things that the kids needed. Before the loss of our son, Jane was a very good and loving mother to the children and a very beautiful and loving wife as well.

I didn't have any idea what was wrong with her, and I was caught up in trying to make a living for us all. There was no one we could turn to for help. I couldn't get her to go see a doctor. I tried time and again to get her out of the house.

Then, some twenty years after Donnie's passing, I came home after a long, hard day's work. She told me she wanted me out of the house. We had not been communicating for a long time. We both had given up on trying to talk. I left and wished later that I hadn't. Another lesson learned is to not be too quick to react.

She then moved back to Rockford, close to her mom and dad, brothers and sisters. We divorced in 1984. This is another one of my greatest regrets.

I am telling you this part of my life because I know there are millions of people who can relate and are having it just as hard as we did.

Later, I learned about depression. I realized that Jane likely had a severe case of it. However, through all those years, I did what I have always done—work, work, and work.

All my life, I never took time to get into sports, fishing, or hunting with my children. I guess you could say I was in a kind of depressed state myself. All I could think about was trying to get more for my family.

I wasn't able to get nice clothes for my children. Since I knew how children at school had taunted me, I knew it was happening to them too. I always felt bad about it because, as I was growing up, I mostly had hand-me-down clothes. If the clothes were still wearable when I grew out of them, my brothers got them.

Are you living this kind of life, friend? Or have you had this kind of hardship? Be of good cheer. There is hope. Despite all the problems I have had, I never thought of myself as having it any harder than anyone else. I have always believed there was someone else who was having a tougher time than me. That is still my outlook on life. No matter how difficult life is or how sick I get, I believe there are others who have it tougher.

My philosophy in life is, "Do my best, and God will do the rest."

But when I was making bad decisions, I thought I was doing the right thing. It's like when you are traveling and come to a fork in the road, and you don't know which way to go. So you try one way, maybe driving several miles before discovering it was the wrong road. You turn around and try to get back to the other road. I have gotten on the wrong road many times in my life—I call it sightseeing—but each time it costs something.

Now a flash back to 1961 for the brighter side of the story when we got saved. Looking at the other side of things, when we gave our lives over to God, things got somewhat better, but were still very hard.

I met a man working in the shop that was very likable. Then I learned he was the pastor of a small church. After a period of weeks, over which he asked me to attend church, we decided to go. God had already preconditioned our hearts.

Jane and I had been talking about going to church for some time before this. We by then had five children, and we wanted to bring them up to know God.

I started taking my family to church. Jane and I gave our lives over to the safekeeping of God through Jesus Christ. The blessing of God began to come into our lives, but I could not see how good it was at that time. I now know that, in life, we sometimes don't notice the blessing because of all the hardships we are enduring. It's called life. But looking back on time passed, I can really see what God had done for us.

I now know why so many people just give up and turn to other things, like drinking and drugs, to help them cope. Without God, that may have been me and my family. I now understand that God had been there all the time. His angels have been by my side from my beginning. I believe this because I had what a lot of people didn't have—a praying mother and father, as well as praying grandparents. Without God, we likely would have just given up, as so many people have.

I know that hundreds of thousands of people have lived lives just as hard as I have, and some had it harder. Can you see what God is doing for you? Even if you haven't turned to God, He is still waiting for you.

Think back on your life. Can you remember some incidents of what you could call miracles? My first time to really understand the real love of Jesus was when I had a dream so real that I can even now see it plainly in my mind's eye. This dream, no doubt, was brought to me because, at some point earlier in my life, I had read the story of Shadrach, Meshach, and Abednego being cast into the burning furnace in the third chapter of Daniel.

However, I don't believe things just happen. God sent me a message. This dream was so real that I could feel the heat from the furnace. I was the one to be thrown into the burning furnace. I looked into the fire, and I saw the face of Jesus. I looked into His eyes, where I saw and could feel such great love that I shook off my captors and jumped into the pit with Him. I felt the heat of the fire for a very short instant. I awoke, and for some time, I lay awake thinking about this seemingly real happening.

My lesson was that there is nothing to fear in death, and His love is so great that I cannot describe the feeling. I now know that God reveals Himself to us.

> He reveals deep and mysterious things and knows what lies hidden in darkness, though he is surrounded by light. (Daniel 2:22 NLT)

And I can still feel that great feeling of the love I saw in the eyes of Jesus. I have felt this same special love on two more occasions.

# 10

## My Shop Years and Miracles

In 1958, I was employed by Rudy Manufacturing Company of Dowagiac, Michigan, and they were later bought out by Sundstrand Corporation. My time working in the shop included some amazing, answered prayers.

God opened many doors of opportunity, supernaturally, for me to achieve promotions without formal training. I was able through the Holy Spirit, to solve problems that others had trouble with. This helped me to be promoted beyond my wildest imagination!

Over the next thirteen years, I went from a laborer to a supervisor. This was such a big deal because of where I had come from: the oldest of nine children in a very, very poor family with a mother who had only a third third-grade education and a dad who had less and was not able to read. He could barely print his name. I quit school when I turned sixteen and went to work full-time in the cotton fields to help my parents take care of our family.

The point here is that I had no skills or confidence in my abilities. I didn't know that I had any kind of talent other than doing what I was told to do.

I had a bad case of an inferiority complex. At that time, I was unable to speak up if I was in a group of four or more people. I didn't feel that I was smart or that I could do much of anything on my own. So after I gave my heart to God, I did a lot of praying, and I depended on God to help me. He never let me down.

Always fearful of losing my job, I never complained about anything I was asked to do. At this point in my life, I thought I was blessed just to secure this lowly laborer job in the maintenance department of a large company. I was very thankful just to have a job so I could feed my family.

I have always been a hard worker, and my bosses noticed me. Soon, they asked me to do the jobs that others would grumble about. At the time, I did not associate the story of Joseph with what I could become.

In the book of Genesis, chapters 39–42, God gave Joseph favor in the eyes of his superiors, and he went from being a slave to the overseer of the whole kingdom. God was giving me favor in the eyes of my superiors. I went from a low laborer to a supervisor of a crew of men in the maintenance department over the next few years.

It all started one day when there was a big rainstorm. A significant leak developed in the roof over some expensive equipment that was getting damaged, and we had to cover it. I asked the foreman if I could go up on the roof and repair the leak.

He looked at me like I should know better and informed me that it couldn't be done because the rain was still falling. I then told him that, before I had moved to Michigan, I had worked for a roofing company and knew some things about repairing roof leaks. I said I believed I can do it in the rain. He said, "I don't believe it, but go ahead and give it a try." The water was coming in in a big way.

What I knew about tar roofing was that, if you can use a torch to heat the tar, it would melt, run into the break, and seal the opening. It was a very big roof, but I knew how to find the leak area. The trick was to stop most of the water from running over that spot while I was melting the tar, but that was simple to do.

I got a piece of two-by-four about six feet long, laid it on the upper side of the break, and told my helper to stand on it to divert the flow of water. I stood over the roof break, an area of about four inches, to keep the rain off that spot while I worked, and in about five minutes, it was done.

Later, Fred, my foreman, walked by the area where the leak had been and found that it was not leaking even though it was still raining outside. He came over to me and said, "I didn't believe it was possible," and offered a few more complimentary words.

I informed him that it was just a temporary repair and that I would need to make a permanent repair when the roof was dry. He gave me permission to do that.

Later, he asked me about my roofing experience. I told him I had worked with a roofing company for a while. He relayed the information to the plant engineer, a man I came to care a lot about later, by the name of Bill, a very foul-mouthed man.

He came by one day and asked about my roof knowledge. After we talked for some time, he asked if I would be willing to check the entire roof over because there was a good number of leaks. What I didn't know at that time was that this would lead me into a full-time job.

In the late fall, when the time came to lay off all the temporary summer laborers, I was fearful all day long. Near the close of the day, Bill came to where I was working, and fear ran up my spine for I was sure I was to be laid off with the other laborers.

But to my great surprise, he asked if I would take a position as a maintenance helper. Of course, I would. That gave me a job and a twenty-five-cent per hour raise.

I had been told by my boss that I could spend any amount of time I needed to do the roof repairs. On the good days, I stayed busy making repairs, and my boss noted over a period of time that there were fewer roof leaks. This set the stage for my next step up.

The following spring, the company decided to build an addition to the plant covering about a half-acre of land, or about twenty thousand square feet. They hired a retired contractor to do the work, and I was placed under his supervision. I enjoyed being out in the sunlight.

God gave me favor in the eyes of my new boss, and he began using me as his go-to man and to tell the other men what he wanted them to do. I encountered some resentment from some of the men, but I did the best I could.

I really began to understand for the first time that God was on my side. I seemed to be a fast learner, and I had gained construction experience while working as a laborer some years back. By this time, I was a Christian. I didn't at that time realize that I had the ability to do what I was doing. I prayed often, and God was my teacher.

Once we had some of the roof decking on, Bill came inquiring about what was needed to install the new roof. He was satisfied that I could do what was needed and then asked me if I would be willing to supervise the installation of the new roof on the addition. He gave me permission to order all the equipment and supplies I would need and told me to pick the men I wanted to help me. Again, God had given me favor with the young men that I had been working with. I had by then been working with all of them for quite some time.

This was a big deal for me. I had never had this much responsibility before in my life. I was very apprehensive and prayed daily for God's help.

These young men with no knowledge of roofing made it very hard for me, as they did a lot of horsing around. I was continually cautioning them about the dangers of hot tar. Then one day, someone accidentally overturned a two-wheeled cart at my feet that we were using to haul hot tar. As it flooded around me, I stepped back and fell backward into the spreading pool of hot tar. Two of the young men grabbed me up out of it and rushed me to the hospital.

I HAD JUST GOTTEN OUT OF THE HOSPITAL
MAYBE TWO DAYS BEFORE THIS.

Tar was covering part of both arms, my legs, and my back, and it had splashed onto my face and other places. Several spots resulted in third-degree burns, and I have the scars to prove it.

While in the emergency room, I heard the doctor say he was not sure how to remove the tar. I told him Vaseline would dissolve it, so he called for Vaseline and began spreading it on. He had to send someone to the drugstore to get more.

The doctor later told me he was amazed at how calmly I had talked with him because I was in shock at that time. I don't remember all of what I said. I didn't know I was in shock.

I think I had to spend one or two nights in the hospital. Then later, after I was home, some of the young men on my crew came to see me while I was recovering, telling me they were amazed at the way I had reacted in this situation.

Previously, they had fun razzing me when I would talk to them about Jesus, telling me they were going to get a soapbox for me to preach from. It was all in fun, and I was not offended. One young man came to see me separately after the accident and told me how sorry he was for his part in making fun of me. He said I had proved I was a Christian by my actions in the emergency. He said they were all frightened, but I was calm—and that helped calm them.

I believe this was because of my dream that had prepared me for the ordeal. I didn't have any thoughts of dying even though many people have died from these kinds of burns, because of blood clots.

Now the roof was nearly completed, but in need of being closed off to avoid damage. A week later, I went in to talk with Bill and told him I could come in and complete the project if he would let me. At first, he said no way, but after I explained how I could get it done; he reluctantly agreed. He instructed the men to build a portable tent and a pallet of cardboard for me to lay on the roof that could be moved as the work progressed. They treated me like a king. God was with me, and we completed the project successfully.

After this, I was respected as a Christian by most of the maintenance men, even my foreman Fred and Bill. This earned me another promotion up to a Class B maintenance man.

# 11      *Special Project*

S ometime later, while I was still just a Class B maintenance man, Bill, the plant engineer came to see me. He wanted me for a very important job building a machine that he had designed. It would take about four months to complete. Out of all the maintenance men, he picked me. I was amazed and fearful that I would fail.

Some of the men in the maintenance shop razzed me about being the boss's pet, and one tried to get me in trouble by telling lies about me. All of them knew I was a professing Christian. This one man told the other men he had seen me out with a woman other than my wife. I called him on it, and he swore it was true. I didn't get angry. I just told him that he was very much mistaken for I had never been with any woman other than my wife. He called me a liar. I simply said, "God knows, and many here know you are telling a falsehood." This man became my personal devil to keep me humble.

Now, I was thrilled at this honor of being asked to head up this new project. However, I was worried as I didn't think I would be able to get it done. It required welding and other skilled work in which I had no experience. Bill stopped by to check on the progress many times in a week. I did a lot of praying.

Somewhere along the way, Bill stopped by and said, "Oh! You are now a Class A maintenance man." I was thrilled for that was another pay raise that I desperately needed.

As we neared the end of the machine-building project, I knew that a lot of electrical wiring would need to be done. At that time, I had done some very minor electrical house wiring while working with a contractor, but this job required more than a minor wiring job. So I thought Bill would bring in an electrician to do that part.

To my surprise, this didn't happen. He laid out a wiring plan called an electrical schematic. I had no knowledge of schematic reading. I was shocked that he was asking me to do this. I said, "Bill,

I don't think I can do this." But he had more faith in me than I did. He said, "You can do it."

So, like I did with everything I was asked to do, I went to work on it. Bill was a good man to work with for he explained each step in detail. I lived in fear and apprehension, and this kept me very humble.

Now, Bill had a really bad habit of using very bad language in every sentence. One day as we were nearing the end of project, with the wiring all done, it was time to fire the machine up. It ran, but not like it was supposed to.

Bill started ranting, cussing up a blue streak because something wasn't working right. He was not cursing at me; he was mad at himself because his wiring design wasn't right. I was fearful that I may have made a mistake, but he assured me that I had followed his instructions.

In one of his silent moments, I said, "Bill, do you really have to use all those bad words?" Now, I had for some time been praying and asking God about how I could talk to Bill about this. I was afraid he would remove me from the project. However, I decided this was something I had to do.

To my amazement, he looked at me and said, "Albert, I'm sorry. I've been talking this way forever, and I forget you don't like it." I said, "You are using God's name in vain, and I feel bad that you do that. You know I'm a Christian." He said, "Yes, and I'm a Catholic."

Thinking I might still lose my job, I pressed on. I said, "Bill, there is a difference between being a Christian and being a Catholic. I know that Catholics go to a priest and tell him they have sinned, asking him to forgive them. That is a good start, but no man can forgive a person's sin. Only God can forgive; we need to ask God's forgiveness."

Most Catholics, as I understand, are baptized as babies and then are deemed Catholic. I told Bill that my wife had been a Catholic when we married, but that she was now a Christian. I said that each person must ask God to forgive them for their sins and be born again by faith in Jesus.

I told him that I had repented by getting on my knees and asking God to forgive me and let the blood of Jesus cover my sins. I also explained what it means to be born again.

> Jesus replied, "I tell you the truth, unless you are born again, you cannot see the Kingdom of God." (John 3:3 NLT)

Then I asked him, "Have you ever personally asked God to forgive you? Have you ever asked Jesus to come into your heart? That is when you become a Christian by faith. You need to humbly ask God for yourself."

He didn't seem to get mad at me, and I don't remember him cursing in my presence anymore.

We finished the project, and the machine worked like he had wanted it to. He seemed to be very happy with what I had done, thanking me many times. And I, of course, was very thankful that God had helped me all the way.

Some weeks later, I was passing by his office, and he called out to me, "Albert, come in for a few minutes." I walked in and was surprised and puzzled when he said, "I did it!"

I said, "Did it?"

He said, "Yes! You know, you told me what I should do to become a Christian!"

We talked for quite some time, both of us were thrilled. I left his office rejoicing, thanking God for his salvation.

A few weeks later, Bill, came by where I was working on another project and told me that I was now an electrician. I was very excited. God had worked another miracle in my life, more money, plus other electricians had electrical schooling, while I didn't. I was not even able to read an electrical schematic, however I took a course in schematic reading later. I don't know how God did it. I was on cloud nine!

The sad part of this story of Bill's life is that after a few months, Bill had to do a company mandated physical. They found out he had throat cancer. The short story is that within 4 months he passed away. I was so thankful that God had allowed me to spent time with him. I became an instrument to lead him to Jesus.

After the death of Bill, the factory hired a new plant engineer named Milton. God gave me favor with him; we hit it off real well right from the start.

Many months later, I was promoted once more to a position as an electrical troubleshooter. This was the top skilled position in the Maintenance Department. This meant that in the eyes of the plant engineer, I had the ability to make repairs on any machine in the entire plant and was trusted to make sure all went well.

Fred, boss of the maintenance men, started getting requests for me to work on things in the front office. This was great because I got acquainted with all of the office staff and had the opportunity to talk to them about God's goodness.

It all started when I had gone to the front office to talk to a lady in the personnel department. In our conversation, she told me about one of her machines that was not working. I happened to notice a wire that had come loose, so I reconnected it and that took care of the problem. This started the ball rolling.

After that, I was called up to the office many times. As far as I know, I was the only electrician ever called to the front office on a trouble call. Previously, they would call in outside technicians. I learned the names of all of the front-office employees and was able to call them by their first names and witness to them. In fact, the financial comptroller and I became good friends for more than twenty years, even after he retired.

Now, this was a big factory with over twenty-five hundred employees, including thirty-some maintenance men and six electricians. For me this was a very big deal. I was amazed and thought, this is as good as it could ever get. I couldn't stop praising God! I could hardly believe I was so blessed, because I had grown up on a farm and had no experience in anything mechanical or electrical.

But time after time, I looked at a machine with an electrical problem, having no idea what was wrong or where to look and God gave me the ability to make the needed repairs. I would stand in front of the control panel and pray that God would help me. Then I would shake something, and some part would fall out, or a wire would fall loose in my hand showing me the problem so I could make the repair.

Another important point is that if you want something from God, ask, and then make a good-faith effort to do something. God always expects us to try, then He makes it happen. If I had just stood looking and done nothing, nothing would have happened. If you want something from God, you must take the first step. Ask, look for what you asked for, and expect an answer. Each time I found the problem, and made a repair, it was a God-made accident for me to solve.

Of course, as time went on, I learned about electrical issues, as one would expect, and then I began finding problems on my own. God was training me and had given me an understanding of how things work. Then, many of the issues were repeat problems.

God never failed me. To this point, I had never gone out to a troubled machine and failed to find and fix the problem. Then came an *exception*.

It was another great learning experience. This machine had developed a problem that created some concerns. It was a very big machine. The electric panel was about eight feet wide, two feet thick, and seven feet high with twenty-five or so relays. There were maybe two hundred wires, a lot of which ran from the panel to the huge machine.

It had an intermittent problem in that it happened only occasionally. Sometimes, it would run for days without stopping, and other times it would malfunction twice or more in a week. This was a big problem for the company because the machine produced copper tubing for the entire shop. Each time it stopped it was time-consuming to restart it.

When I was sent out to work on this machine, as I always did,

I prayed, asking for God's help. But this time, I didn't receive it. I wondered if I had failed God in some way. Did I not have faith? What had I done wrong? However, as I learned later, God had it all under control.

I learned another very important lesson: If you don't get an answer to your prayer, don't despair. God has something better lined up for you. After all the electricians had taken a shot at finding the problem, Fred, the foreman, Milton, the plant engineer all looked this machine over for a few weeks or more and did not find the problem. The plant engineer decided to call in a manufacturer representative.

The representative shut the machine down and proceeded to check it over. After he worked on it for some days and watched it run with no malfunctions, he gave up. He could not identify a problem that did not exist at that time he was there. He said he would return if there were more problems. Nothing happened for a while, and then it started malfunctioning again.

Now, I'm not telling you this to brag on myself, but to give glory to God for His answered prayer.

# 12     *How God Intervened*

I was asked to work on the night shift for one week. The usual night man was out on vacation, so I had more time to just stand, watch, and pray. I did what God expected me to do, kept praying. One night, the machine malfunctioned again. I stood there for maybe two or three hours studying, thinking, and praying.

Here comes the miracle.

I accidentally leaned against a cable that ran from the control panel to the machine while it was running, and it malfunctioned again. When the machinist got it set up and running again, I reached over and shook the cable and lo and behold it malfunctioned. Now, I had an idea that the cable was the location of the problem. There were maybe fifty control wires that ran to a part of the machine that moved up and down.

I asked the department foreman to shut the machine down, and within a few hours, I had it going. *God had come through for me again.*

I found a wire that was broken. It made just enough contact to let the machine run, only losing contact occasionally. I ran a new wire on the outside of the cable, solving the problem. The next day I reported to Fred that I had found the problem. I gave all the credit to God for my discovery. He had heard this from me before and believed it.

Some weeks later, Milton, the new plant engineer, came out to see me and said, "The VP wants to talk with you." He took me up to his office. The VP told me he wanted me to take a position as maintenance supervisor for the second shift.

I told the plant vice president that I didn't feel I had the ability to handle that kind of job and that I had just signed up for an adult education class. He said, "Great! Just what I wanted to hear. You go to that school on company time." He added, "I know you can do the job or I wouldn't have asked you."

To my surprise, the schooling was very easy. I believe that God and His angels were with me the entire time.

I got along very well with most of the maintenance men, except for the one who was my personal devil. He continued his rebellious ways. One Saturday, he came in drunk and was belligerent. I had no choice but to have security escort him out of the plant. He later went to the union and claimed he had not been drunk, and his fellow union workers would not support me. The security guard did, but the company did not want the fight, so they paid him for the day's work. Milton, my boss, agreed that I had done what needed to be done.

Most of the time, it was an OK job, but the union made it difficult. Sometime later, the company began to go downhill because of union troubles. Over the next three or more years, the company decided to move to Mexico. I was laid off in 1974, along with about twelve maintenance men.

I had decided to start a construction business, and just as I was getting it going, I got a call asking me to return as supervisor. There had been an accident in which a large piece of equipment had been damaged.

I didn't want to return, for I knew it would be very temporary and I had a few projects going. I was asked to talk with the VP, and he asked me, "How can I get you back for the few short weeks that it will take to repair the equipment?" He said, "I need you." In short, I couldn't turn him down. I talked with the people with whom I had projects going, and they all agreed to wait or get someone else to do their project. About four weeks later I finished the Sundstrand job.

I returned to my business, and I kept my guardian angels busy. Once, I fell from a two-story building that was about twenty feet high, and only broke two ribs. I had stepped onto a ladder, and it moved sideways, causing me to fall and hit the edge of the roof, I fractured my two ribs.

The miracle came in with one of my beloved sons, Stanley, who was standing below saved me. Because God gave him fast thinking, he ran up behind me and pinned me against the building wall, breaking my fall. Without him, I would have bounced back and slammed my head on the cement.

Another time, I fell from a big barn roof, only suffering bruises. I have fallen many times, once even hitting my head on a cement wall. In a snowstorm, my car slid off the road and hit a steel post. I ended up with only bruises, while the car fared less well.

God has saved me so many times. Wow!

# 13

## Strange Encounter in the Shop

One Saturday, as I remember it, the shop was empty except for security personnel. The only way a person could get in was by signing in with the guard at the gate or having a key to the front office.

I was walking down an aisle from one area to another when I met a man coming toward me from the front office area. He was not dressed like most of the office people that I would see from time to time. He was dressed in casual work clothing—something like what I was wearing.

However, from the moment we met and as we talked, I began to feel this deep feeling of joy in my spirit that was so unusual. I had never met anyone who gave me this kind of feeling before. It was similar to the feeling in my dream when I saw Jesus.

As we talked about the goodness of God and about Jesus, I was elated and amazed at some of his words. I noticed a strange thing later as I thought back on the conversation: I could not remember things that he said. We had talked for some time, and I was so interested that I had forgotten I was on a tight schedule. The machines in the shop had to be monitored twenty-four seven. For some of the machines, it was critical that they be checked hourly.

I needed to move on, so we each spoke words of blessing for the other. I walked away for about ten steps or fewer and turned to look back at him. To my shock, he was gone! There was nowhere he could have gone so quickly. I thought it was strange but did not think about it anymore at that time. I figured he surely was employed in the shop somewhere, or the office, and that I would look him up and continue our conversation later.

I had never thought about meeting an angel.

For the next few months, I searched the entire shop and office. I never found him. I couldn't get him out of my mind, and still to this day, some sixty or more years later, I can still see him coming toward me with his big smile and love on his face.

Much later, as I continued thinking about him and praying, I concluded that I may have met an angel because of things that were taking place in my life. Much later, I remembered this story from the Bible:

> As they talked and discussed these things, Jesus himself suddenly came and began walking with them. But God kept them from recognizing him. (Luke 24:15–16 NLT)

> As they sat down to eat, he took the bread and blessed it. Then he broke it and gave it to them. Suddenly, their eyes were opened, and they recognized him. And at that moment, he disappeared! They said to each other, "Didn't our hearts burn within us as he talked with us on the road and explained the Scriptures to us?" (Luke 24:30–32 NLT)

# 14 *My Church Years*

et me take you back to about 1961. I was so excited about what God was doing in my life that I thought I might be called to preach. I took an online Bible knowledge course and a course to become a licensed minister in the denominational church I was attending, which included taking a six-week class at a church seminar. Later, I started going to a nursing home—back then we called it an old folks' home—where I got permission to conduct a monthly meeting. With my Bible and my guitar, I gave a talk about the saving power of Jesus, read a few scriptures, and sang a few songs. Then I spent some time visiting with some of the residents. I tried working at a nursing home again in 2018, in North Carolina. But my health was not up to par, so I couldn't stay with it.

THIS WAS AROUND CHRISTMAS 2018

Also, back in 1961, I was asked to start a mission in a very small town some miles away. I have always been the kind of person to do my best at whatever I am asked to do. But with no financial help, plus working long hours, the situation was just not good for any of us. And the small town did not have a volume of people to work with. I worked at it for less than a year.

Later, I was asked to move to Grand Rapids, Michigan, to start a mission and build a new church there. The state association agreed to pay all my moving expenses, make the payments on an old store building, and pay for supplies I would need to rehab the building. This was in the fall of maybe 1967.

But I still had to work at a full-time job to support my family. Plus, I needed to remodel the building to convert it into a decent place to bring people to our new church. This was a two-story building in a residential neighborhood, maybe thirty feet by eighty feet.

I decided to move my family into the upper area, but I had to make it livable first. There was about three feet between this building and the neighboring buildings on each side. The lower part was about twenty feet longer than the upper, so there was no backyard for the kids. The back of the upper part had an open porch area of about twenty by thirty feet. I installed a railing around it and trusted God and the obedience of my children to keep them from falling off.

As soon as I could take time, I spent one evening of the week and most Saturdays visiting people around the neighborhood. God blessed my labors, and by Easter Sunday of the following year, we had over one hundred people show up—standing room only. For the rest of the year, we averaged fifty or more per week.

I was putting all my efforts into the work that I had before me. I had committed for one year. After seeing how hard it was on my family, I decided not to stay for the second church year. I told my wife that if I could get my old job back, I would move back to Dowagiac. This was before the plant made the decision to move to Mexico. She was thrilled at the idea of moving back to Dowagiac.

I made a trip back to check on the possibility at my old shop job. As I walked into personnel, my old boss Milton was standing there.

He gave me a handshake, and the first thing he said was, "Are you coming back?" I said, "If you will have me."

He turned to the personnel director and said, "Put him back on the payroll." He turned back to me and said, "When can you start, in the morning?"

"One week," I said. I got my old classification of electrical troubleshooter back. God's great blessing one more time.

I drove from Grand Rapids to Dowagiac and back, approximately ninety-five miles one way, five days a week for the next two months until my church assignment ended. You know that was a difficult thing to do, but God was with me all the way. I found a place to live back in Dowagiac just before the church year ended.

# 15

## My Falling Away from God

Sometime in the mid-1970s, the pastor of the Dowagiac church resigned, and I was asked to take over. I did, and things went well for a couple of years.

Then one day, a young man started coming to our church. I knew that he was a member of the same denomination from a few miles away, but I didn't think much of it, figuring he just wanted to help us out because we were a smaller church. He stayed a little over a month and then stopped coming.

In a few weeks, I received a letter from the state overseer telling me I had been accused of preaching heresy. I was given a date and time when I was to appear for an inquiry by the elders. This shook me up. I was in shock and couldn't believe my eyes. I couldn't imagine who would be making this charge. I was in tears for I had tried so hard to stay within the guidelines of the church.

A few weeks before this, a fellow pastor and I had made a trip to the denomination headquarters. We were inquiring about a certain scripture that the church was using that didn't make any real sense to us. I thought this might be the reason for this examination.

On the day that I was to show up, I was stressed out big time. When I went into the meeting, I saw that the young man who had visited with us was there. But it didn't occur to me that he would be the one making the charge.

When the meeting was called to order and the charge was read to me, I nearly fell out of my chair. It was this young man who was making the charge of heresy. As the overseer read the charges, I was more shocked about what he had done. He reported some statements I had made, but left out some of my words, changing the context and meaning of what I had said.

I then told the board what I had said and what I had meant. After a little while, the young man started vigorously defending himself by saying that I was changing my story, and he got more agitated. Finally, he took from his billfold his minister license from the denomination, threw it on the table, and stormed out of the building.

His pastor was one of the men on the elder board. He turned to me and said in a very harsh tone, "Now look what you have done!" This cut me to the bone. The overseer dismissed the meeting, and no one said anything else to me.

I cried all the way home. The more I thought about it, the more I hurt. I had no idea if they all thought I was wrong. I was devastated. Nothing had ever hurt me as much as this. I had put my heart and soul in everything I had done. I tried praying, but it seemed as though God had deserted me.

I discussed this with some of my church members, and they were upset as well. Sunday came, and I still hadn't heard from the overseer. I had no idea if I was still the pastor or not. And I was in no state of mind to stand in front of the members. One of my deacons, along with some others, told me I should skip the morning service. So the call went out and there would be no service that day.

I waited till midweek for a call from the overseer. Nothing.

Once more in my life, I acted too hastily. I sat down and wrote a letter resigning my position as pastor, sending my minister's license to the headquarters of the denomination.

The assistant overseer got word that I had resigned and sent the young man who had started all this over to pastor what had been my church. This was the move that destroyed me completely.

The young man came over and talked with all the members. The second Sunday after this, he came with a good number of young people from his church. I don't know how many of the local people came. But within two months, this young man gave it up.

The state overseer finally called, telling me he would be stopping by to talk. I agreed to meet with him. We talked for quite some time, and he apologized for leaving without talking to me at the close of the meeting. He said he thought I understood that I had done nothing wrong.

When I told him what the assistant overseer had said, he then understood why I was so hurt. He did more apologizing, but I just couldn't get past my hurt. So, I refused his request to return to the ministry one final time.

So, within two months or so, they closed the church for good, never to be opened again. I was bitter, and I seemed not to be able to pray.

I now felt like the ignorant kid who had left the farm in 1951, despite all God had done for me in the years since then. I wasn't looking back and counting my blessings. I was looking back and carrying my hurts around.

# 16    *Deep Fall into Sin*

ow, I tell you the following story to once again point out this can and has happened to many good, God-fearing men and to stress that sin is sin. It doesn't matter how great we think a sin is. Any sin separates us from our loving and forgiving Father.

In 1985, I met a realtor who needed a carpenter. She was in real estate and owned two to three fixer-uppers. She was a beautiful blue-eyed blonde. I was smitten from day one. She explained that she didn't have enough money to pay for what needed to be done and asked if I could work something out. Later, I realized I should have run from that woman right then.

I took on the first project with a promise of payment within thirty days. She was a sweet-talking saleslady. I should have been alarmed. But I was blinded, and at this point in life, I was alone and lonely.

I had become a pretty good carpenter over time, and she needed someone with my abilities. She poured on the honey, and I ate it up. Over a period, she bragged on how great I was. She offered me a partnership because I had the ability and the means to do the work she needed to have done.

After a time, she told me that she loved me, and I was smitten. I thought I was in love as well. I fell like a rock.

We agreed to get married, but she didn't want to set a date yet. We talked about our partnership that she was to put in writing, but she didn't get it done. Each time I would inquire about it, she would offer the excuse that she was so busy that she just hadn't had time. Then, she said, "We will soon get married, and we won't need the written agreement." I fell for that story.

The devil gave me the illusion of a happy life to come. So, fool that I was, I moved in with her. I became a lowdown sinner and really hated myself. I was now at the bottom of the barrel of sin as far as I was concerned.

Over the next nine years, we never got married for she always had an excuse. She had, though, managed to get everything into her name, including my contracting business. I never knew about most of the dealings because I was working ten to twelve hours a day, seven days a week. We had built a net worth of over a million dollars.

By this point, however, I was very miserable living the life I was living. I could see it was never going to turn out well. Like before, I had put heart and soul into this, and I could see no way to get out. Then the bottom fell out from under me.

When I began praying again, asking God to forgive me and to help me, this time prayer seemed to be working. I cried, "O, my dear God, I have gotten myself into a mess. I don't know how to get out of it. Please, God, help me." He came to my rescue in a way I couldn't have imagined. She found a man who had a lot of money, and she then dumped me. I found out that I didn't own anything anymore. Then I went and had a long talk with her new friend. He told me what she was telling him, That I was just a friend helping her. I then went to a long-time lawyer friend. He was shocked; he had thought we were married.

In short, we fought it out in court, and I lost it all. The judge gave her everything except the house I had before we had gotten together. He gave me nothing for my years of labor because she claimed to have paid me by giving me a place to live. So that was room and board, plus she had given me spending money and had bought me a new pickup truck.

I had gotten the notary she named in court, and he testified that he had not signed any of the documents. Yet the judge gave it all to her even though the judge recognized that she had forged my name and the notary's name on several legal papers. She was well connected in the political arena.

Afterward, her new friend dumped her. She later paid a very big price for all of her lying and cheating. On a sad note, she did not live to enjoy any of the spoils. A few short years later, I got word that she had ended her life while sitting in a nursing home, staring out of the window.

I didn't rejoice over her death. I only thanked God that I could forgive and forget and move on.

# 17 *Repented and Redeemed*

I repented, asking God to forgive me, and was so thankful to be free again and back in God's loving embrace. I didn't cry or mourn my loss. I had paid a great price for my stupidity and never once wished for any of that money. I asked God for His forgiveness, and I know He gave it for He said he would, and I believed Him.

Later, looking back on this, I couldn't understand how I could let God down this way, for He had done so many miracles in my life. Then the Holy Spirit came on me and brought back to my memory how the Israelites, God's chosen people, failed time and again. He did miracle after miracle for them, and still, they fell back into sin. Well, so did I.

However, I could not forgive myself. I started going back to church, but I couldn't get up and speak because I didn't feel worthy.

Now, I tell you that I am blessed, and no matter what I have done. God has always blessed me despite all my dumb decisions. The whole point of this book is to tell you that, whatever you have done in life, God will forgive you. You have hope until you take your last breath.

God prepared my life going forward. Fast-forward to 1995. The kids had all grown up and moved away. God started blessing my life again, giving me more property. I started dating a good Christian woman and married her in 1998. Life was good again.

I was faithful in church, doing what any Christian was expected to be doing, mowing the lawn, and doing other needed work—except I couldn't do anything that required me to stand up and speak in church. I just couldn't forgive myself, for I was so ashamed. I felt so unworthy.

I had a long talk with my pastor, and he told me the things I already knew. Yet I just couldn't make myself get up and talk before the church people. I was only what I called ankle-deep in God's great Spirit. I didn't have the zeal I once had.

Later, I understood that I hadn't prayed through it yet. Yes, I was praying, but I hadn't spent enough time asking God to cleanse my conscience.

Then in 2004, the church was having a business meeting, and a heated argument started. For some reason and without even thinking, I stood, shocking myself and the whole church, and offered a resolution that settled the conflict.

After that, I was able to speak and sing from the podium as though nothing had happened. I had won victory over my loathing guilt.

In early 1999, I had to have quintuple heart bypass surgery done, then the next year I had shoulder surgery. Again, God took me through it.

I confess that I don't know why except to say that He loves me, and maybe He was not done with me yet.

When I was discharged, I was told that most heart surgery like mine would last anywhere from twelve to fifteen years, then I would have to do it over again. My roommate was on his second go-round.

As far as I'm concerned, I had another miracle: I am in my twenty-fifth year with this bypass. Praise God!

However, I have had some tough times. In 2011, I had a very bad time. I suddenly started getting weak and ended up falling a few times. When I fell once, I hit my head very hard on a cement block wall, then laying on the ground and couldn't get up.

My primary care doctor and my cardiologist were both baffled. My primary care doctor sent me to a neurologist. The only thing he found was that I had a back problem that I already knew about. But he did not think that contributed to my falling problem.

In 1956, I found out that I had a birth defect. I discovered this when I could not get out of my bed one morning. I ended up in the hospital for two weeks. They found I had this birth defect with my sacroiliac, and I ended up having to wear a back brace for six months. I was told at that time that I would likely be in a wheelchair by the time I was fifty or sixty years old. Praise God—I am now eighty-nine years old, and God has kept me free of a wheelchair.

However, this birth defect wasn't why I was so weak and falling at this time. My primary doctor sent me to an eye, nose, and throat specialist to see if it was a balance problem.

But that doctor found nothing that was causing my falling. This had been going on for about four or five months. My blood pressure would change from high to low then back to high all day. When was low, it was like 65/45. The lowest times, of course, were when I would fall. I fell four or more times in one month.

One day I woke up in the morning with a headache. As the day progressed, my headache worsened to the point that I couldn't keep my eyes open. Aspirin hadn't helped, so I went to the hospital late that evening. My blood pressure was 220/100-plus. I hadn't gotten any better, so I began thinking I was about ready to leave this world, and at that point I didn't really care. My doctors were baffled. I went home with no answers.

Then a strange thing took place.

I was sitting in my recliner one day. I don't know if I was asleep, or not, but suddenly, a woman was standing in front of me handing me something. I raised up to take whatever she was holding out to me. As I did, she disappeared. I looked over at my wife, who was asleep on the couch. I woke her and told her what had happened.

When I went to my next doctor's appointment, I told him about it. He said it was most likely a hallucination from my medication. However, an amazing thing was taking place. I began getting stronger from that day on and was back to my old healthy self within two months.

I believe I had seen an angel.

Then in 2013, I had a minor stroke. After a short time, I recovered. In 2014, we moved to North Carolina, and my health was great. We bought a house, and I did a lot of remodeling on it. Then, we bought another fixer upper that I remodeled. We sold both houses and bought another fixer-upper in the Leland, NC, area, and I rehabbed it as well. I was in good health for about five years after the vision incident.

Then in 2017, I had a heart attack and needed a stent and a pacemaker with a defibrillator. In early 2018, I believed once more that I was dying as I got weaker each day, to the point of not being able to get out of my chair without help, just like the 2011 affliction.

This was when I got, I believe, another visit from an angel of God. I was sitting in my recliner, and again, I'm not sure if I was asleep or awake. However, I heard a firm voice saying to me, "If you don't get moving, Nancy (my wife) will come in and find you dead." I opened my eyes, expecting to see one of my neighbors.

*No one was there*, yet I knew I had heard that voice loud and clear! Believers may say it was an angel. My doctor again said it was maybe a hallucination from my medications. But if that were the case, why did it not occur more regularly? I had been on these medications for a number of years.

Regardless, I got up and started on the road to recovery by walking. Within two months, I was back to my old self and walking one or more miles most every day.

In 2019, I began to feel the need to do something, but I couldn't explain why I was restless.

Now for another sad part of my story. It started with my wife and I having a disagreement. I began believing very strongly that God had something He wanted me to do, but I couldn't find the words to tell her, because I didn't know what it was. All I knew was that I was very restless.

I am truly sorry for my part in this breakup. I have asked God for His forgiveness for my part. I tried to talk to her about it, but she refused to talk, telling me I was stressing her out.

So I gave up trying and went over to Tennessee. I have four sons there, and I could keep busy while trying to find out why I was so restless. My health was good, so I kept doing different projects, including buying another fixer upper.

Later when I met the angels, I believe I found the mission God wanted me to get busy with. This book project is what God was trying to get me to do. From that day on, I have been busy trying to be a witness for God, and to work for Him by trying to be a blessing to others as you will see in Chapter 20.

# 18 Getting Old!

As you may know, it is hard to admit that you can't do things you used to do. In 2007 and 2008, I climbed up Superstition Mountains in Arizona on a trail up to a place called Flatiron, a nine-hour round-trip climb that was enjoyable with a beautiful view. So I thought I could do it again. In 2020, on my eighty-sixth birthday, I was feeling good and planned to try climbing the trail up to Flatiron again. I believed I could do it.

So I made the trip to Apache Junction, AZ. My one and only aunt lived in that area, so I made the trip for a visit and to climb that mountain. I got there two days early so I could climb some lesser trails first.

On October 9, I climbed a trail that was a three-mile round trip. I had no problem. Then on October 10, I did another trail that was five miles round trip and had no problem. I was confident I could do the ten-mile round trip to Flatiron and back.

However, it was harder and steeper than I remembered. I stopped to rest several times. About halfway up to Flatiron, I got to an area that was very steep, about 125 feet or so, up to a less hard climb.

But this turned out to be my undoing.

I got about three quarters of the way up this steep, nearly smooth rock area when I realized I wasn't going to make it to the top. After resting for some time, I decided to return to my car. But when I turned to go back down, I slipped, fell, and then rolled a short way before I could stop myself. I had lost some hide and hurt my left shoulder badly, and I couldn't get up. God came to my rescue one more time by sending what I like to call an earth angel. An earth angel, in my opinion, is someone who comes to another's aid without expectation of being rewarded, like in the Bible story called the Parable of the Good Samaritan in the book of Luke. This man came and helped me get up, and then he helped me get down the steep area.

God had another earth angel there who was with the sheriff's department's search and rescue team. He helped me climb down to an area where they could get an ATV up to me. We rode the ATV the rest of the way down. When they got me to my car, two deputies were there to interview me. They told me they were required to make a report on any injuries because the area is a federal landmark open to the public.

I thought I would be rebuked for my foolish idea of trying to climb this mountain at my age. Instead, they praised me for trying, saying that at least I hadn't quit living. Now, I have never been accused of being smart. The only real smart thing I have done in my life was to call on the name of Jesus, not asking for justice, but asking for mercy.

# 19         *Mystery Man*

od reminded me of a song that was given to me by a stranger: "Go tell the world they are lost without Jesus." This song came to me in a mystifying way.

In 2013, my wife and I were having a garage sale. She had gone somewhere, and I was sitting in the garage with my guitar, playing and singing. A man walked up, so I stopped playing. He asked me to continue, and I obliged him. After I completed my song, we began a conversation about music and the different songs we liked. He then said that he wrote songs and said, "I have four songs I want to give you."

This by itself is strange. Why would someone who didn't know me come prepared to give me this gift? He didn't live in this city.

He went back to his car and shortly came back with four songs. One was titled "Who Rolled the Stone Away," another was "Builder," the third was "Go Tell the World They Are Lost without Jesus," and the last was "One of These Days."

I thanked him, and he told me to use them in any way I wanted to. I replied that I would like to have something in writing authorizing me to use them. He said he didn't live in the area, but that he would send me a letter. To my surprise, in a few days, I received a letter giving me 100 percent ownership of the songs.

This was a very strange mystery. We lived in an area with one way in and one way out. Why would a man be out traveling around prepared to give away some gospel songs? People don't just drive around in an unknown area looking for someone to give songs to like this, unless it was a gift from God.

As I have stated before, I don't believe in coincidences. He had to have planned to do this beforehand. I have no idea where he lives.

I still have three of the original songs on his original sheets of paper. I spilled coffee on the other one, destroying it, but I have a copy. I thank God for this gift, but I didn't understand how I was to use them, for I'm not a gifted singer.

I now believe it was to be used in my latter days project, in my work for God playing and singing before those that are in need of a word of cheer, See Chapter 20.

Now, as for my feelings about music, it is special to God and to me. Music reaches into the heart of God and His people. I love the old country gospel songs that tells a story and that ask salvation questions like, "Are you washed in the blood, in the life-giving blood of the Lamb?"

I also love songs of praise, like "I Feel Like Traveling on and On" and "Oh, How I Love Jesus," and songs of prayer, such as, "One Day at a Time, Lord" and "It's Me Again, Lord," which has the line, "I have a problem I can't solve." Then there are songs of looking forward, like "There Will Be Peace in the Valley" or "Just Inside the Gates of Heaven," just to name a few.

Music—oh, how sweet it is.

I have four sons who play musical instruments, and I feel so blessed. I was at a church service some years ago. A man played a violin so beautifully, I was almost brought to tears. As I watched and listened to him play. I suddenly saw a faint light that I had not noticed before shining on him. In my mind's eye, I could see an angel with his arm around this man's shoulder. It was such a fantastic out-of-the-ordinary experience that I had to tell him. I didn't know him at that time. I later learned that he was a good friend of my sons, and now he is my friend. I love him just about as much as I love my sons.

Praise God, and glory to Jesus Christ, my Lord and Savior. I am striving to do what I wholeheartedly believe He is asking me to do. Throughout this book, I use the term "I believe" to convey that I am doing what I know God has revealed to me. Another term I often use is "I want to believe," which suggests "I hope." This means that I am not 100 percent sure whether a thought originated from God, from just myself, or, God forbid, from Satan.

One thing I do know is that, if what I am thinking fits the Spirit of God's word, I can't be too far off. And I now always ask God to confirm if what I am thinking is what he wants me to do, as you will see later.

This does not suggest I'm a know-it-all, as I'm not! After all these years, I'm still learning. I'm doing my best to do what I know and believe God has shown me for this part of my life. I haven't reached the state of perfection, and I don't expect to until I cross over to the far side with Jesus.

> I don't mean to say that I have already achieved these
> things or that I have already reached perfection. But
> I press on to possess that perfection for which Christ
> Jesus first possessed me. (Philippians 3:12 NLT)

I have learned another valuable lesson: Make eye contact with those with whom you are talking. Eye contact is a very important aspect of nonverbal communication that is recognized not only throughout the human world but in many species of animals as well.

I love talking with people on a one-on-one basis. Doing so, I have been blessed in such a great and marvelous way that I don't have words to express my joy. I have found that, by making eye contact, I can feel when I relate to that person as a real friend. There is a difference between just talking to someone and being connected to someone in a truly loving brotherly or sisterly connection.

To my wonderful family and friends, I feel the need to keep moving and keep witnessing to people, for we all need a word of hope. For what God has done and is doing for me, He will do for you. Most of us may think we can't do much of anything. However, *all things* are possible if you just say, "I will try."

I'm not skilled with words, and I'm not brave. I don't have the ability to articulate a rehearsed speech well. I have only one thing going for me, and that is understanding that my hope is in asking for and believing the Holy Spirit of God will fill my mouth with the words He wants me to tell someone.

The devil wants me to believe I have no ability to do anything, but like I have always done, I just say, "I'll try." He wants me to believe that God has deserted me because of all the physical things I am allowed to endure.

And yes! Even though I have hurt many people because of my ignorance, I have asked for God's forgiveness, and He has given it. I don't expect all will forgive me, but that becomes their burden, not mine.

Read Matthew 6:14–15 (NLT): "If you forgive those who sin against you, your heavenly Father will forgive you. But if you refuse to forgive others, your Father will not forgive your sins."

As I said earlier, I was born with a back problem. Now, it is to a point where I just fall over backward. I seem not to have any control; if I stand still for a short time, I just fall. Although I don't always fall to the ground, for I have learned to stand where I can get a hold of something.

The fallimg started mainly in 2011, with about four falls per year. In 2021, the falls resulted in two concussions. Three or more years, 2022. Now in 2023, the falls keep coming. No matter how careful I am, I just lose it. This is not a complaint. One day I will fall into heaven.

I have asked God to heal me. He hasn't done it yet. Now, of course, Satan is trying to make me believe that if I was God's son, He would heal me.

Here is what he said to Jesus: "During that time the devil came and said to him, 'If you are the Son of God, tell these stones to become loaves of bread' So I don't fall for that lie about "if I'm God's son," for I know who I am.

But I remember that many followed God with greater handicaps than the little ones that I have, like Job, the prophets, and others throughout the Bible. I remember Steven's being stoned. I remember Paul's having an affliction.

> Three different times I begged the Lord to take
> it away. Each time he said, "My grace is all you
> need. My power works best in weakness." So

> now I am glad to boast about my weaknesses, so
> that the power of Christ can work through me.
> (2 Corinthians 12:8–9 NLT)

The old devil can't make me feel sorry for myself. For I understand that God created me with a divine, self-healing body. What He expects from me is that I pray, asking Him to give me wisdom as to my health care, and that I do my part by loving myself, eating healthy, and exercising. When I do find I have a particular medical problem by going to the appropriate medical doctor to whom God has given the skills to care for that ailment.

Some people don't want to take the help that God has provided for them. Some say, "I'll wait for God to heal me." This makes me think of the old story of a man on the rooftop of his flooded house, praying for God to save him. Along comes a boat whose driver offers to take him to safety. He says, "No, thanks. God is going to save me." Then a helicopter comes to his aid, but he still refuses to go, saying, "God will save me."

He dies in the flood. His soul goes to heaven, where he asks God, "Why didn't you save me? I believed and had faith that you would." God said, "I sent you a boat and a helicopter, and you refused them."

I had a good friend many years ago who didn't believe in going to doctors. His church discouraged its members from seeking medical attention. They taught divine healing only, saying people should just trust God. He got skin cancer and suffered for months before he died.

I visited him many times, watching him in agony, and tried to talk him into going to a doctor. He said, "No, God is healing me." Finally, he started saying he would rather not talk about it. It was so sad to see. However, he held onto what he believed to the end. Do I believe that God could have healed my friend? You bet I do, but God wants us to do our part.

I must keep on keeping on! I have this very deep desire to keep looking for places to tell my story. I'm reaching more and more people with my witnessing. I'm increasing the number of friends, brothers, and sisters who are praying for me as I keep on keeping on. It is such a joy to connect with loving people.

So I don't worry about what anyone will say or think. I just witness. I thank God for it because I have never in all my years been any happier with my life than I am now. God will let you know what He wants you to do. Ask Him.

He has said in His words, "For many are invited, but few are chosen" (Matthew 22:14 NLT). You are invited to say, "Here I am, Lord!" Do you want to be a chosen one? I believe God is calling you. If you accept, you will find great joy and unspeakable and full glory.

At the start of my mission, not knowing just how to get started, I said, "Lord, I have heard you say, 'Witness,' but how, Lord? I just don't know how to reach people." In our culture today, it seems people don't want to talk about their faith or talk with strangers, especially about religion. But I heard again, "Witness!"

After a few weeks of praying, I believe He gave me some answers. I got what I believe was an inspired idea and put together some wording to print on business cards. I was not sure if it was proper wording, so I didn't do anything about that idea for some time.

Again, on another day, I was walking at the dam and praying, and once more, I heard, "Witness."

I then said, "My Father, please confirm to me if I had the right wording, you would want me to use." Within fifteen minutes, I got my confirmation by meeting a very special person.

As I was leaving the parking area, a woman and her nephew were walking in the middle of the road. I stopped until she saw me. I pulled up beside her and said, "Good morning."

She said, "I'm sorry. I was praying with my nephew and didn't hear you."

I said, "That's OK. I was praying as well, and I'm not in a hurry." We talked for some time, and then she asked what I was praying about. She said she would pray in agreement with me. Then I told her I had a strong feeling God had told me to witness but I wasn't sure how, so I thought I would have some business cards made.

The front side would read, "Prince Albert in the Kingdom of God." To the right of "Albert," I would have a crown to remind me that I am a son in His kingdom. On the left side would be a cross to remind me that Jesus said to take up our cross and follow Him. The back of the card would read, "Don't forget to show hospitality to strangers, for some who have this have entertained angels without realizing it" (Hebrews 13:2 NLT).

The woman said, "Yes! Oh, yes, that is a great idea. I wish you had them now; I would love to have one."

This is when I decided to use the name Prince Albert that many of my friends had called me.

We continued our conversation, and I found that she didn't live in this area. In fact, she had never been there before. She said she had heard about this dam and decided to check it out. Some would say it was a coincidence that she was at the dam at the same time as me; but I don't believe in coincidences.

> The Lord directs the steps of the godly. He delights
> in every detail of their lives. (Psalm 37:23 NLT)

> The LORD directs our steps, so why try to understand
> everything along the way? (Proverbs 20:24 NLT)

I have heard it said that coincidence is God's way of being anonymous. This had to have been a God arrangement.

I got the business cards made and now call them my witness cards. They are working better than I could have dreamed they would, and I have been amazed at the great responses I get. Most times, when I give out a card, the other person and I get into a wonderful conversation about God and His angels. I now say when I hand a card to someone, "There is an interesting story behind this card."

One morning, I met a very interesting couple by the name of Paul and Esther. We really connected. Right from the "hello," I could feel their warm, loving personalities. I told them I believed God had called me to witness and of my meeting with what I believed were two angels and why I thought so. I saw and heard no doubts from them.

They told me they had been praying for a way to open a dialogue with people to talk about God. I gave them a handful of my cards and said, "Just tell them about meeting me to open your dialogue."

They were thrilled and said, "We will never forget you!" I replied, "I won't forget you either." We did the three-way hug, and it was wonderful, full of love—but not like the hugs of angels. We had a wonderful prayer time right there in the parking lot.

Another day, I saw a young woman sitting on the hood of her car. I gave her my card, and we talked for a while. I could see she was very troubled. Just as I was ready to walk away, I asked, "Is there anything I can do to help you?

She said no, so I turned to walk away but she called out to me, "Yes." I returned, and she told me a sad story. I prayed with her, and I then could see a smile on her face. She gave me a big hug and thanked me for caring.

Since I started this, I have had many people ask me to pray for them and with them. I recently met a nurse, and as I was telling my story, she suddenly said, "Please pray for me. I am taking a trip, and I would love for you to pray for a safe journey for me." I did at that very instant. Many volunteer to pray for me that I will be blessed in my effort in witnessing to people, telling them about God, Jesus, and His angels.

I have given out cards to and shared my witness with my doctors, law enforcement officers, and many others. Most tell me how much they appreciate me for doing that.

Walking has become a real blessing for I have gotten to know and have made many friends. I love when people witness to me about what God has done for them.

Another time, I was walking at the dam with a new dog. (I gave her away after this.) She ran in front of me, and I tripped over her and took another nasty fall. Ouch! I lost some skin and bruised a rib. However, God turned this into joy for me.

A woman who was nearby came to my aid. I want to call her an earth angel as well for not only did she help me up, she assisted me back to my car a half mile away. We talked about the goodness of God and about our Lord and Savior, Jesus Christ, for quite some time. Then we prayed for each other. I'm praising God that I didn't suffer greater harm.

I didn't understand why I kept falling. I walked outside my house on Sunday, June 6, 2021, and when I turned to go back into the house, I was surprised to find myself lying on the cement in front of my car. I had fallen backward and hit my head very hard once again. Short story—I spent three days in the hospital. I kept asking, "My Father, God, why? Why does this keep happening to me?"

Now, I'm not saying God told me the following. However, I have been thinking about how the early Christians and Christians of today all over the world are suffering because of their faith in our Lord Jesus. If God is allowing these things to happen to me as a witness to those around me, then I am happy to suffer with them. Mine is nothing compared to what others are going through.

I have never complained about my heart-breaking injuries, but I have told of them as part of witnessing. In each of these falls, I have had the joy of meeting wonderful people and witnessing to them. This last hospital stay gave me time to meet and witness to many nurses, and I found most of them to be loving children of God.

Then in November 2021, I fell while standing and talking with a woman I had met. I just fell backward for no apparent reason. I was on the grass and had no injuries. Then again, on January 2, 2022, I was standing and talking to a man when I suddenly fell backward. This time, I was on a gravel driveway and lost a lot of skin on my left arm. This was when I went to see my doctor to tell him there had to be something wrong other than me being careless.

Doctors found I have spinal stenosis of the lumbar region, whatever that is. I was told this couldn't be helped with surgery. The best I can understand is that, if I am standing a certain way, my legs go momentarily numb, and I just fall backward. God never promised me a bed of roses. But His Son, Jesus, said, "Take up your cross and follow me."

I can show you by my sins a loving God who forgives. I want you to understand that you're not lost. There is a loving God just waiting for you to call on Him. Make your decision today. Why wait? You may wait too long. He gave you the right to choose heaven or hell.

As I started writing down the things God brought to my remembrance, I was surprised to see that my life has been filled with miracles from the day I was born. This is the answer to the question of how to witness for me: "Go tell the world they are lost without Him."

For anyone who knows me, I am the last person in this world who would think I could or would write a book. Even I am shocked. I don't have the ability to articulate well, and I'm not good with spelling. But God makes the impossible possible!

I was blessed and protected while I was yet a sinner and when I was a worthless Christian. God's angels have been by my side for He knows how much I need His help. I believe God is trusting me to be His witness and has given me the Holy Spirit to comfort me in all my suffering so that I may tell of His glory and be a witness to what He can and will do for those who believe and have faith in Him.

He said, "Seek the Kingdom of God above all else, and live righteously, and he will give you everything you need." (Matthew 6:33 NLT).

I started the year of 2021 with a desire to get back into church. I hadn't been in church for most of 2020 because of the pandemic that had kept most churches closed. I started going where one of my granddaughters attends. I was blessed in the church, and I loved the people and pastor. However, it was quite a distance away from home.

One day, I was passing by the entrance to a church near home, and the thought came to me to check this one out. I walked in and was warmly greeted, and after the service the pastor came over right away and greeted me heartily. Other members did as well. This was a church that had a lot of amiable people. I have made many lifelong friends.

My prayer is that this book will be a source of inspiration to take you on a deeper walk with God. I pray this book will work its way around the world before the end of the age. May God be *your* God and Jesus *your* Savior, the Holy Spirit *your* Comforter, and His guardian angels *your* safety net.

Remember this, we win in the end:

> But you belong to God, my dear children. You have already won a victory over those people, because the Spirit who lives in you is greater than the spirit who lives in the world. (1 John 4:4 NLT)

Thank you for reading my book. It is my prayer that something in it spoke to your heart. I believe this is a call from God telling me to tell you that He loves you and I love you.

I will be giving away as many copies of this book as possible. I am trusting God to supply the funds. I know God has many people willing and able to make this a real success.

God's miracles in my life are ongoing yet today. My hope is that you will be able to relate to my story in some way. I love meeting new people who share their stories with me.

I once talked with a man and woman who were doing missionary work somewhere in Africa. They were back in the States because the man had to have heart bypass surgery. They told me about their work over there and how God had blessed them, including a story about a miracle they experienced with another missionary while still in Africa.

They said they were out riding and passing a vacant lot that was for sale. The man's wife said, "Stop. I feel God wants us to get this property." He told his wife that they could buy it, but then they wouldn't have the money to build a church. He told me it would cost about five thousand dollars to build a small building on the lot. However, she believed God was telling her to get it, so they bought the property.

Then another day, they were in a different area, and the same thing happened again. So by faith, they bought the second lot. A few weeks later, they were in a little church service with only a few people there. When the service was over, they stayed to help clean up the church. While the wife was cleaning the altar, she saw an envelope. Upon opening it, she found a note and ten thousand dollars in cash. The note said, "Build the two churches." All the people had gone, and only the pastor and the couple were there. They had done by faith what He laid on their hearts, and God did the rest.

God will provide whatever is needed to get done what He wants to be done. All He needs is someone with faith willing to try.

No, it's not our good works that get us to heaven. It's our faith along with our good works. Strive to become an earth angel.

> What good is it, dear brothers and sisters, if you say you have faith but don't show it by your actions? Can that kind of faith save anyone? Suppose you see a brother or sister who has no food or clothing, and you say, "Good-bye and have a good day; stay warm and eat well,"—but then you don't give that person any food or clothing. What good does that do? So you see, faith by itself isn't enough. Unless it produces good deeds, it is dead and useless. Now someone may argue, "Some people have faith; others have good deeds." But I say, "How can you show me your faith if you don't have good deeds? I will show you my faith by my good deeds. You say you have faith, for you believe that there is one God. Good for you! Even the demons believe this, and they tremble in terror. (James 2:14–19 NLT)

I believe God called me, and I accepted my assignment to witness for him. Are you willing to accept your assignment? He is offering one to you.

Jesus said, "Take up your cross and follow me." My cross? Yes, it will get heavy at times, but the times of joy wipe out the times of pain. It's like a woman having a baby. The pain must be almost unbearable at the time of delivery, but a few days later, the joy of the new baby has wiped the memory of the awful pain into the far background.

I'm not saying I enjoy the pain—no way. What I enjoy is what God does with it. I'm not implying you will have to suffer anything, for God deals with us all in different ways.

I'm an alien in this world, and it is not my home.

> We are here for only a moment, visitors and strangers
> in the land as our ancestors were before us. Our days
> on earth are like a passing shadow, gone so soon
> without a trace. (1 Chronicles 29:15 NLT)

A church song reiterates this, saying, "This world is not my home, I'm just passing through. My treasures are laid up, somewhere beyond the blue."

I want you to know that you are unique, one of a kind. There is no one like you in this world. Have you ever thought, *who am I? What is the meaning of life? What am I here for?* Most people have pondered these questions at some point in time.

You are a spiritual being living in a temporary shell called a body. You came from God, not from your mom and dad. They made the shell you function in, the body. Your body is made of earthly material that will decay and pass away. But you get to decide if you want to go back to be with God for all eternity or stay somewhere else. God only wants those who want Him.

You get to live for a few years with no worries as a child. Then one day, you have to make decisions for yourself. Life gets very complicated.

You learn early in life that there is good and evil. You learn there is a yes and a no to every decision you make. You learn that

God created you and loves you and wants you to spend eternity with Him. You also learn that Satan wants to keep you and offers you many pleasures to stay with him. You are faced with a hard decision: pleasure now for a short time or pleasure later for eternity.

Many choose to wait for later in life so they may enjoy the pleasures Satan has offered them in the present. However, as it turns out, what was offered was a deception. There was no lasting pleasure. As the years go by, you search for this elusive pleasure, and it can't be found. By and by, you fall deeply into this hell on earth.

Some just give up rather than turn to God. Many make the decision to end their lives rather than humbly choose God. Some, because of their reckless lives, die in the pursuit of this illusion.

There are only two types of people on this earth. You are either a saint or a sinner, heading for heaven or hell. You are either on God's side or Satan's side—nothing in between. The sad part is that you didn't choose to be on Satan's side. But when you didn't choose good over evil, you have chosen evil by default.

God will not force humans to serve and love Him; He gives us an alternative. He wanted us to love him because we want to love Him. There is no love in captivity. That is why God gave you the right to decide for yourself.

You were conceived in sin because of Adam's decision to disobey God. From that time on, every person is given a choice. You must make a conscious decision to take God's side or stay where you are. No decision is a decision. If you have answered His call, then you are no longer a part of this world, but you are in Kingdom of God.

> The world would love you as one of its own if you belonged to it, but you are no longer part of the world. I chose you to come out of the world, so it hates you. (John 15:19 NLT)

However, if you have not answered His call, you are still a part of this world and have no excuse if you end up in hell.

> For ever since the world was created, people have
> seen the earth and sky. Through everything God
> made, they can clearly see his invisible qualities—his
> eternal power and divine nature. So, they have no
> excuse for not knowing God. (Romans 1:20 NLT)

I have heard people say, "How can I believe in something I can't
see?" Well, many things are invisible. No one can see the wind, yet
you believe the wind is real. Why? You can feel it; you can see the
evidence. No one can see the spirit, yet you see and hear the evidence
of it when the spirit comes into the body of a newborn baby. This
spirit is forever; it will never die.

Understand this: no baby is condemned to hell until God is sure
that the child is old enough to know right and wrong. God knows
our thoughts and the intent of our hearts. God gave every human
being a sense of right and wrong, an awareness called a conscience
so no one will have an excuse.

> Even Gentiles, who do not have God's written
> law, show that they know his law when they
> instinctively obey it, even without having heard
> it. They demonstrate that God's law is written in
> their hearts, for their own conscience and thoughts
> either accuse them or tell them they are doing right.
> And this is the message I proclaim—that the day is
> coming when God, through Christ Jesus, will judge
> everyone's secret life. (Romans 2:14–16 NLT)

But you will live in heaven or live in hell. You get to make the
judgment call. Death is only for the earthly body—from dust to dust.
You see the evidence when the spirit leaves the body. That person has
departed to heaven or hell! The body goes back to the dust of the earth.

From the time of accountability until just before the end, you
can make the decision to go to heaven. Remember: No decision is
a decision.

> Don't copy the behavior and customs of this world, but let God transform you into a new person by changing the way you think. Then you will learn to know God's will for you, which is good and pleasing and perfect. (Romans 12:2 NLT)

Think of that—you can become a new person! If you let God have complete charge of your life. He will transform you into a powerhouse. As a part of His kingdom, you have unlimited power; you just have to learn how to use it. All things are possible:

In a Bible story about a boy possessed by an impure spirit, the boy's father asks Jesus to heal him.

> So He asked his father, "How long has this been happening to him?"

> And he said, "From childhood. And often he has thrown him both into the fire and into the water to destroy him. But if You can do anything, have compassion on us and help us."

> Jesus said to him, "If you can believe, all things are possible to him who believes." (Mark 9:21–23 NKJV)

As to being unique, we are told there is no other person in this world that has the same fingerprint as we do. Think about that! Only God can perform this kind of miracle. Of billions of people, each has a distinct print. God also has a unique purpose for you if you will accept the assignment.

God loves all people who come into this world and is trying to help you see what you can inherit. He enlists the help of all of those who have made the decision to join Him. These people, filled with His great love, are willing workers trying to help nonbelievers see the light.

As to being from the throne of the kingdom of God, we are

spirits inhabiting bodies. The life in you is an unseen spirit. I know
for I had an out-of-body occurrence in which I was above my body
by what I guessed to be about eight feet, looking down.

> Then the LORD God formed the man from the dust
> of the ground. He breathed the breath of life into
> the man's nostrils, and the man became a living
> person. (Genesis 2:7 NLT)

This planted a seed that forever reproduces itself. Each new body
created is given a spirit, "you." You came from God, and you are a
God spirit that could become a good spirit or a bad spirit. A spiritual
being is the life in that body.

God did not make us robots but in His image. He made us
spirited with free will to choose. Even the angels have free will. We
can live a life of joy with Him or a life of misery.

I highly recommend that you find a church that teaches you the
truth as it is written in the Bible. A church that teaches about who
God is, His Son Jesus, the Holy Spirit, the power of God, and how
you can use this power.

Get involved. God is calling you and has a purpose for your
life. Check it out to see what God has in store for you. I am happy
in the church I am attending and feel loved by all. One big thing
that stands out for me is the love I see on the faces of the people.
Most make eye contact and give big smiles. Eye contact during a
conversation is vital. Friend, I want you to know the importance of
looking into the eyes of those with whom you are conversing with,
for it is said that the eyes are windows into the soul.

Eye contact is the way to make the best of friends. With eye
contact, you can learn what people are thinking about you. It can
also either support or discredit the words you say. This means a lot.
Another song I love is titled "Blessed Assurance." Some of the lyrics
are as follows:

This is my story, this is my song, Praising my Savior all the day
long. Perfect submission, perfect delight. Visions of rapture now

burst on my sight; Angels, descending, bring from above, Echoes of mercy, whispers of love. Perfect submission, all is at rest, I in my Savior am happy and last, Watching and waiting, looking above.

This story is my reality. Please don't judge me until you have studied and prayed. All I ask is that you pray about it, ask God, and follow Him. People found fault with God, Jesus, and everything else; I don't expect the people of the world to be any less hard on me. Anyone can become a critic, but it takes a loving, caring, compassionate person to live up to the standards set up by a loving God.

Therefore, as the elect of God, holy and beloved, but on the tender mercies, kindness, humility, meekness, and longsuffering; bearing with one another, and forgiving one another, if anyone has a complaint against another; even as Christ forgave you, so that you also must do. (Colossians 3:12–13 NKJV)

# 20 Last Chapter of My Life

After my visit with the angels in 2021, I asked God what he want me to do. And as noted in the that section of this book, I kept hearing "witness." Over time I began trying to think of what I could do. I remembered how I had played and sang in the health care centers. I thought I might do that again as I once did. I even believed God told me he would send me a helper. I was hoping to be a blessing to the souls there that needed encouragement and the love of God.

I had visited a few places in Tennessee trying to get started in my music ministry. I believed that this is what God wanted me to do. I found that because of COVID 19, the health care centers were not allowing people in to minister to the residents. So, then I returned to working on this book again while waiting for the opportunity to return to my music ministry.

Over time I got to a point in my life where I was feeling so weak that I couldn't get around well enough to live by myself. My daughter, Kathy, came to visit me in Tennessee where I was living. She stayed with me for a few weeks and saw how I was struggling to get around. She asked me to move to Indiana to live with her and her family, so I moved to Lafayette in August 2022.

After I got settled in with my daughter, my health seemed to improve. I went looking for a health center where they would allow me to come in and entertain those lovely people. I did an hour program with my daughter's help. The people there seemed to love my southern gospel songs. But I was too optimistic about my health. When we got back home, I got out of the car and fell backwards in the yard, and I couldn't get up even with my daughter's help. She had to go find a neighbor to help get me up. I discovered when I fell I had hurt my back. It took three weeks to get over that injury.

I went back to the health care center and set a new date to

return to do a second performance. The morning, I was to be there I developed a problem and ended up in the hospital. So, I went through another bout with Satan working me over. At this point I was beginning to think I could be wrong about what God was wanting me to do. Over the next few weeks, I was weak and no matter how much I prayed I was not getting healed. Don't think for a minute I doubt God's healing power. He can heal me of all my afflictions in an instant. But sometimes God allows us to walk through a valley for a season before we can go to the mountain top.

God has always turned my sorrows into joy. My job is to keep faith. He will not let more come upon me than I can bear. As I read through the Bible, I find many stories about people that had a very hard time before victory came. I remember all the trials that King David went through, Daniel in the lion's den, Stephen who was stoned, and Paul had very hard trials before he was martyred. God carried them all through, and I know He will do the same for me. In the end will I win. Read the last two chapters in the book of Revelation.

I believe I now understand why God has allowed me to go through these trials. It was to get me into the place and time where he wanted me to be for this end of time. Let me tell you about the next big miracle in my life. Some months ago, I went to church one morning hurting so badly that after I was there for a while I decided to go back home. A lady saw that my head was down in agony and suddenly she came up to me and put her arm around my shoulders and prayed for me. I was surprised, but as she prayed, I began to feel relief and my pain subsided somewhat. I didn't notice what she looked like. During the start of the service the pastor made an announcement for people to pray for those who needed healing, and that same lady was back again to pray for me, so this time I thanked her.

Next time I was in church I was feeling much better. I eventually got the chance to talk with the woman and tell her how much I appreciated her prayers. Over a period of time, we developed a friendship. God has allowed us to spend time together and what I discovered about her shocked me. The woman is the most perfect Earth Angel I have found in my life. I have known hundreds of great people that qualifies to be an Earth Angel. I have written about my definition of what an Earth Angel is earlier in this book. The goal should be for all Christians to be Earth Angels serving one another, but only a few of us ever reach that goal. Read Luke 10:30.

This woman has a love for people, she is a humble person that has a very tender heart showing compassion, kindness, and patience for others. She has wisdom and is a prayer warrior. A friend to all and loved by those that know her. And her son and daughter have the same spirit in them. I have never been treated better than I have by her family. I told her what I had hoped to do at the health care centers. I was surprised she had the same hopes of doing this same kind of work for God. I found that the church had scheduled regular programs of singing and entertaining the residents in the nursing homes by a wonderful person that had been doing it for many, many years. I volunteered to help and was accepted. I love working with these two great wonderful spirit filled women of God.

So, God has opened the door for me. My dreams have come to pass – Praise God! I believe God is going to bless me in this work, and He is answering my prayers. Here I am 89 years old playing and singing southern gospel songs with my 12-string guitar. As we entertain the residents, we feel their love and appreciation. God is still doing miracles in our lives.

He has answered my prayers. One more time after some months of working together the one I called "The Perfect Earth Angel" consented to become my wife. This fulfilled the word God gave me when He said He would give me a helper.

Friend, God will do miracles for you too. Just say, "God, here I am, lead me on into your will and your work." What He has done for others, He will do for you too.

I hope you found more to love in this book than you found to dislike. My prayer is that this book will have been a source of inspiration to you to take a longer walk with God.

I would love to know; this work is going around the world. Tell your friends on your social media about me, Prince Albert, and about what God has done for me. Tell them about this book, which will be available as an e-book at a very low cost.

Remember, there are no do-overs in life! You can be as happy as you choose to be.

# 21 *Conclusion*

For every hurt I have had over the years, I have suffered patiently, and God has made them into joy for me. If you have suffered some hurt, look for what He has done with it, or will do, if you want Him to. Just ask. God will turn your heartaches into joys, and your troubles are only temporary and will go away.

There is a song titled "One More Valley" that I love to sing that goes like this:

> When I am tossed on life's seas, and the waves cover me.
>
> And dark clouds won't let the sunshine through.
>
> Then a voice seems to say, child; there will be a brighter day!
>
> Don't let the dark clouds hide heaven's sweet view.
>
> You may have one more valley and one more hill.
> You may have one more trial, and one more tear.
> One more curve in life's road, one more mile yet to go.
> Then you can lay down your heavy load,
> when you get home.
> Oh, you can lay down, your heavy load,
> when you get home!

This song tells it like it is!

I believe that certain things have happened to me so I can be a better witness. God didn't cause the accidents. However, He made them into a victory and a great testimony and joy unspeakable for me.

In the beginning, God created me in my mother's womb; then He breathed the breath of life into me, and I became a living soul in this sinful world.

Another song I love goes like this:

This world is not my home; I'm just passing through.

My treasures are laid up somewhere beyond the blue.

When I was twenty-six years old, I made the decision to answer God's call. I answered by repenting and was born again by faith in His Son Jesus Christ, and I became a son in the kingdom of God. I was baptized as commanded by Jesus.

Jesus came and told his disciples, "I have been given all authority in heaven and on earth. Therefore, go and make disciples of all the nations, baptizing them in the name of the Father and the Son and the Holy Spirit. Teach these new disciples to obey all the commands I have given you. And be sure of this: I am with you always, even to the end of the age." (Matthew 28:18-20 NLT)

Being, baptized is an expression of your determination to bury your sinful life, and be resurrected as a new person, born again by faith in Jesus Christ and a child in the kingdom of God. Born once in the flesh to die in this sinful world; born again into the kingdom of God, never to die. Born twice, die once.

I am so thankful for the peace in my heart. I'm ready to go to meet Jesus anytime He calls. When I lay down this earthly body and move into heaven in my new body to never die again, what a joyous day that will be.

Friends, what God has done for me, He will do for you and more. Just ask Him. Trust Him with all your heart. When in need, call on Him in faith. Jesus said, "You can ask for anything in my name, and I will do it, so that the Son can bring glory to the Father." (John 14:13 NLT)

May God be *your* God, Jesus *your* Savior, the Holy Spirit *your* Comforter, and His Guardian Angels *your* safety net.

Remember this: We win in the end.

> But you belong to God, my dear children. You have already won a victory over those people, because the Spirit who lives in you is greater than the spirit who lives in the world. (1 John 4:4 NLT)

Life is a gift to you. The way you live your life is your gift to those who come after you. Make it a fantastic one. Live it well!

Enjoy today! Do something fun! Be happy! Have a great day!

If you liked what you found in these pages, please speak about this book on your social media platforms.

I leave you with this prayer:

My Father, I ask your blessings for my family and friends, and for my friend who is now reading this book and their families and friends. I ask for good health, safety, and a long life. Dear God, if anyone in these families or friends need anything, please supply that need in abundance so that they may know your great love. If any of them are unsaved, may they ask forgiveness and ask Jesus into their hearts. Dear God, I pray you will have mercy on those who may wait too long. I pray in the name of Jesus Christ, my Lord and Savior, Amen

Know that I care and, most of all, that God cares. If you are lukewarm in spirit, may you rededicate your life, for surely time is very short.

Thank you for reading my book. It is my hope you found something that spoke to your heart. I believe this is a call from God telling me to tell you that He loves you and I love you.

As for me, my best friend is Jesus Christ. I have hundreds, maybe even thousands, of friends. Anyone who smiles at me is my friend; I love you all. With regards to my relatives, my favorites are the ones I am with at any given time. And as for angels, I believe they are always around us.

What if God opened our eyes as he did for the servant of Elisha?

> Then Elisha prayed, "O Lord, open his eyes and let him see!" The Lord opened the young man's eyes, and when he looked up, he saw that the hillside around Elisha was filled with horses and chariots of fire. (2 Kings 6:17 NLT)

God's miracles in my life are still ongoing yet today. Thank God for victory. Soon, you will be able to say about me, "He laid himself down to sleep, and the Lord his soul did take."

Thanks to God, He blessed me with two women in my life who helped make me who I am, good or bad. I am loved by those who mean the most to me, my family. First, my mother loved me even when I was unlovable. ...

Second, Jane, the mother of my children, endured what she could not enjoy. We had many good years.

Also, to my loving family, including my uncle Earnest, my mother's brother; my aunt Frances, my mother's sister; and my brothers, sisters, nephews, nieces, and many cousins, may we all meet in heaven! God has blessed you all. I am so thankful for the times we spent together. Thank you for the great love you have shown me despite my many shortcomings, mistakes, and failures.

Stay well, my children and grandchildren! Live for Christ! You will have *a blessed life* if you are faithful to the teachings of God. It is a miserable life without Christ.

> It's not what you gather, but what you scatter that tells what kind of life you have lived. (Helen Walton)

# One Last Thought

As you know, every so often your computer gets sluggish and needs to update and then reboot. The human brain is the ultimate computer; God programmed it. Every so often it gets sluggish as well. We need an update. This is done by our maker God. How? Through long, deep prayer while He is downloading into it and rebooting you. Then you are good to go again.

If my story has touched you and you'd like to help others find it, please consider leaving a review and sharing your comments with any of the major online book retailers.

# THIS BOOK IS ABOUT

The miracles in my life and
the angels I have encoundered
and to tell the world what God
has done for me. He will do the
same for you. God told me to
witness I said how? He said just
tell what I have done for you.

Printed in the United States
by Baker & Taylor Publisher Services